The
Form
of the
Book
Book

Foreword

Sara De Bondt & Fraser Muggeridge

The following papers were first presented at The Form of the Book conference on 30 January 2009, at St Bride Library in London. The title is an homage to Jan Tschichold's collected essays on book design, written between 1941 and 1975 and published under the title *The Form of the Book: Essays on the Morality of Good Design* (Lund Humphries, 1991). Tschichold's *The Form of the Book* provides a set of recommendations to produce books that are well-designed and historically grounded. This standpoint is more timely than ever, for despite the technical transformations that have affected graphic design since the original *The Form of the Book* (screen-based interactive reading, instantaneous and affordable full-colour offset lithography, digital printing, print-on-demand, the proliferation of graphic designers and design schools, and ecological awareness), the basic ingredients which Tschichold so lucidly analysed – namely, text and image – remain.

The Form of the Book Book hopes to reignite interest in Tschichold's publication, while offering an alternative to the glossy picture compilation that passes as a reflection on graphic design these days. In contrast to Tschichold's book, however, this one involves a variety of voices – from the young practitioner to the established design historian – and tones – from the conversation to the reminiscence. Yet what the texts collected here have in common is an interest in the book as a material space for critical self-reflection and exchange.

At the beginning of our research we received a letter from one invited speaker: 'I don't really do lectures. I can make my points far more clearly and concisely in writing. It's best just to read the books (...). I don't like listening to lectures much – books are a far better form of communication.' He may have a point: we hope you will enjoy this collection of talks, now available in the form of a book.

5

Le Corbusier as Book Designer: Semi-Modernity *à la française*

Catherine de Smet

The object of this essay is to discuss Le Corbusier's editorial production, specifically from the point of view of modernity. In this respect, and for a number of reasons, Le Corbusier comes across as a particularly interesting case. First, because the graphic output of a celebrated figure in the field of modern architecture is, in itself, worthy of study. Second, because book production played an important role in Le Corbusier's œuvre: he published approximately thirty-five books, which he not only authored but illustrated and laid out, going so far as to choose their format and paper. Lastly, Le Corbusier stands out for having turned his back on his native Switzerland – a paradise of modern graphic design – in favour of France, where he moved in the late 1910s, unambiguously adopting what Robin Kinross in *Modern Typography* terms France's 'marginal' position vis-à-vis the developments of modern graphic design.[1] This marginality is hardly due to ignorance: when Le Corbusier and Amédée Ozenfant founded the journal *L'Esprit Nouveau* (1918–25), the two men displayed a keen awareness – much greater, in fact, than did most in France at the time, even among the well-informed – of foreign avant-garde publications, of the research on the alphabet carried out at the Bauhaus and of the applications of New Typography.

The relatively classical appearance of *L'Esprit Nouveau* reflects exactly the will of its editors, who were otherwise familiar with the magazines documenting the work of the period's great graphic designers – from Karel Teige to El Lissitzky, Alexander Rodchenko to Kurt Schwitters, not to mention Max Bill, whom Le Corbusier knew personally and who edited a volume and designed several dust jackets of Le Corbusier's *Œuvre complète*. In fact, *L'Esprit Nouveau* occasionally published translations of articles that had first appeared in these foreign magazines.

In what follows, I will limit my analysis to certain characteristics of Le Corbusier's book production, which are, on the one hand, highly personal and irreducible to a putative 'French' position. On the other, they are intimately related to a French context – a relation determined in part by the numerous exchanges Le Corbusier entertained with his publishers and a number of individuals who played a key part in the development of his way of producing books.

I will present various examples that illustrate what I would like to pinpoint as Le Corbusier's highly ambivalent relationship to the question of modernity in book design. Before, however, I would like to sketch a chronological overview of Le Corbusier's book production against the backdrop of the architect's overall editorial output, in which books never ceased to occupy a central position. This is, we will recall, the same architect who wrote in *My Work* (his 1960 autobiography written entirely in the third person in which he refers to himself by his initials): 'A large part of LC's creative work took shape in his books.'[2]

Étude sur le mouvement d'art décoratif en Allemagne (1912) is Le Corbusier's first book, published when he was still Charles-Édouard Jeanneret. Visually unremarkable, *Étude sur le mouvement* is nonetheless essential for its content. In it, Le Corbusier discusses the revival of the book in Germany, and in particular his stay in Peter Behrens' studio, whose work as architect, graphic designer and typographer made a lasting impression on him. While *Étude sur le mouvement* was published in Switzerland, the following title – *Après le cubisme* (1918) – co-written with Ozenfant, was published in Paris, where in the meantime Le Corbusier had chosen to settle down.

From 1923, eight titles would follow, all published by Crès as part of a series entitled *Esprit Nouveau*, which Le Corbusier set up to accommodate his own production. The series' title was based on the journal, from which the content of several of these books was lifted. Following Crès' bankruptcy, Le Corbusier would never again entrust his books to a single publisher, but would instead diversify

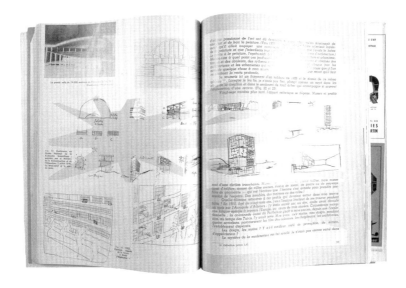

Special Le Corbusier issue of
L'Architecture d'aujourd'hui (1948)

his publishing options to avoid finding himself without an outlet for his projects.

Commissioned by the London-based publisher The Studio, Le Corbusier produced *Aircraft* in 1935. The fee for this commission allowed him to finance the book on which he had been working for years and which he held dear, namely *La ville radieuse* (1935), published by Éditions de l'Architecture d'Aujourd'hui, which had been unable to underwrite the project's total costs. On this occasion, Le Corbusier established *la collection de La Civilisation de l'équipement machiniste*, a new series in which would appear *Des canons, des munitions? Merci! Des logis... SVP* in 1938. The oblong shape Le Corbusier chose for this series – one already adopted for the volumes of his *Œuvre complète*[3] – would once again make it fashionable for architecture books. *Quand les cathédrales étaient blanches*, published in 1937 by another French publisher, Plon, is Le Corbusier's account of his trip to America. The book's subtitle, *Voyage au pays des timides*, refers to the observation the author made upon arriving in New York, that the buildings in Manhattan were not high enough.

Between 1941 and 1946, Le Corbusier produced nine books, despite the difficulties facing the publishing industry in those years. Indeed, it was precisely because he could not produce buildings during this period that it became imperative for him to produce books. He was hardly selective when it came to the political allegiances of his publishers, however. In 1941, Sorlot – publisher of the Maréchal Pétain's writings and of *Mein Kampf* – also published Le Corbusier's *Destin de Paris*, while Gallimard published his *Sur les quatre routes* thanks to the resistant Jean Paulhan. And in 1942 Le Corbusier's *Les constructions murondins* came out, funded by a large grant from the Vichy government.

Exceptionally, the cover of *Charte d'Athènes* (1943) – whose square format Le Corbusier would use again for the two volumes of *Modulor* – bore no illustration, contrary to the subsequent four books on whose covers was a symbol that had appeared a year earlier on *La maison des hommes*. The symbol was designed by Le Corbusier to signify the merging of the architect and the engineer, and its recurrence was intended to emphasise a common identity across the books despite their different publishers.

After the war, two American books came out, in 1947 and 1948. The latter, entitled *New World of Space*, was the first to present in such an inextricable way the two aspects of Le Corbusier's œuvre – his architecture and urban planning, and his artistic production.

Between 1950, when the first volume of his well-known *Modulor* appeared, and 1955, when the second came out, Le Corbusier published the two smallest books in his corpus. *Poésie sur Alger* (1951) sublimates the failure of urban planning for Algiers in a book with a distinct poetic-artistic appearance, while *Une petite maison* (1954) is the first true monographic study devoted to a building, the house Le Corbusier designed for his parents thirty years earlier.

1955 saw the publication by Tériade of *Le poème de l'angle droit*, Le Corbusier's artist's book *par excellence*.

By then the series in which *Le poème* appeared included books by such illustrious artists as Henri Matisse, Pablo Picasso and Fernand Léger, and Le Corbusier was far from insensitive to this recognition of his artistic stature. The luxurious book, or rather portfolio, is the largest of all Le Corbusier's publications. However, consistently concerned as he was to make his work accessible to all – including to 'poor students' – he planned to re-issue it as an affordable bound edition.

Les plans de Paris 1922–1956 (1956) was Le Corbusier's next book. No less than *Le poème*, I would argue that *Les plans* should be seen as a fully-fledged artist's work, under the unassuming guise of an ordinary book printed on plain paper. Finally, his aforementioned autobiography written in the third person came out in 1960. Though published simultaneously in several languages, its primary language was German.

Other groups of printed work should be included in this overview of Le Corbusier's published corpus, including his contributions to magazines, which later fed into his books. Among these magazines I have already mentioned *L'Esprit Nouveau*, but there are others in which Le Corbusier's work appeared in various forms.[4] The eight volumes of the *Œuvre complète* referred to above constitute another such group, just as the books designed from the mid-1950s by Jean Petit, the young graphic designer and editor whom Le Corbusier put in charge of a number of book projects and who would inherit, at the end Le Corbusier's life, numerous documents intended to ensure the legacy of the architect's printed work. To this list one should add the unfinished book projects, as well as the reprints, which for Le Corbusier represented opportunities to rethink the original and which in some instances gave way to unexpected design solutions.

One of these reprints triggered a debate that relates directly to the problematic at hand. In the early 1960s – that is, a few years before Le Corbusier drowned in the Mediterranean at the age of 77 in 1965 – Gonthier, a Swiss

publisher, offered to have several of the architect's titles
reprinted as paperbacks. Le Corbusier accepted, his interest in
encouraging the dissemination of his work overriding, in this
case, the fact that he would not have control over the layout.
Agreeing to the books' reprinting did not mean that
Le Corbusier ceded the right to have a say in their covers'
design. The font chosen by the publisher for this series of
humanities books was a serif with heavy contrasts between
thick and thin strokes, producing a 'classical' effect meant
to soften the negative impact produced by a 'popular' format
associated with works of 'high culture'. The question of the
vulgarisation of the canon was the subject of fierce debate
in France at the time, with some intellectuals going so far
as to denounce it as an act of cultural debasement. In the
face of the pressure exerted by the publisher, for whom all
the books in the series should adopt the same graphic identity,
Le Corbusier stood firm, insisting that the titles of his own
books be set in 'his' sans serif typeface – the same he used
on most of his covers, which he called 'Antique bâton
allongée'. The redundancy of 'Antique' and 'bâton' served
to underscore the importance Le Corbusier attached to the
absence of serif – precisely a sign of modernity in typography.
Thus he could write to the publisher: 'Your books should
have no difficulty accepting that Le Corbusier is modern
(when it comes to typography) while Plato is classical.'[5]
In this tussle with Gonthier, Le Corbusier would initially
have the upper hand: the first two volumes published during
his lifetime came out with titles laid out according to his
specifications. Yet as soon as he passed away, the publisher
modified the books' cover design so that they conformed
to the standard shared by all the other titles in the series.

The sheer volume of correspondence between Le
Corbusier and the publisher on the subject of the books'
covers is testimony to the key role played by typography
in a debate both sides considered critical. In their very
disagreement, the author and the publisher demonstrated
a common awareness of the symbolic power of typographic
design. For the publisher, sans serif type lacked the

'seriousness' to support theoretical texts – a position, however laughable today, that illustrates how conventional the publishing context was in which Le Corbusier operated. Likewise, we can only smile at Le Corbusier's claims in favour of a type deemed modern, particularly in light of his published work where the 'modern' touch is far from consistent, whether in the books' internal layout or on the covers, where the composition remains in most cases symmetrical and classical and where even the sacrosanct Antique allongée appears only intermittently.

Thus one has reason to be surprised by Le Corbusier's inflexibility when it came to the Gonthier covers. But besides his intention to establish his authority and impose his will on his publishers, as he was in the habit of doing, seeing them as mere subordinates, Le Corbusier understood the value – in the specific case of paperbacks issued at the turn of the 1960s – of a 'modern' image. Modernity in graphic design was one possible resource among others: Le Corbusier drew upon a formal repertory, occasionally selecting modern elements when he deemed them appropriate, while remaining open to the possibility of combining them with non-modern ones.

This openness is in fact characteristic of Le Corbusier's approach, and came to the fore very early on in his publishing career. His use of Antique allongée for the books published by Crès in the 1920s aside, it would be another decade before he adopted distinctly modern layout techniques, particularly through photomontage. The first time photomontage appeared was in the highly polemic book *Croisade ou le crépuscule des académies* (1933). As Jan Tschichold observed in his article 'Qu'est-ce qu'une nouvelle typographie et que veut-elle?' published in the French magazine *Arts et métiers graphiques* (1930), photomontage was a preferred illustration technique for New Typography.[6] The technique was, moreover, widely perceived as a vehicle for social and political commentary, a perception theorised by two of the technique's earliest advocates, John Heartfield and Gustav Klutsis.[7] It is therefore not coincidental that Le Corbusier turned to photomontage in a book in which he waged war –

Croisade ou le crépuscule des académies, mock-up (1932–33)

as its title bluntly states – against academicism, and in which
political discourse is deployed with a heavy dose of irony,
reinforced precisely by the use of photomontage. The cover
of *Croisade* itself uses a montage of images, accompanied
by a Gothic script suggestive of something medieval and
retrograde, to mock the conservatism of the architecture
which the book denounces, while simultaneously echoing
the theme of the crusade evoked by the title. The tone is set
from the very first illustration: a photomontage featuring
Le Corbusier in front of a work by Gustave Umbdenstock,
an architect whose designs are the privileged target of the
book's scorn. In the caption, Le Corbusier speaks of himself
in the third person: 'Leaning on the galley's rail, Le Corbusier
thought: light is what must be sought…' Throughout
the book, the illustrations follow this contrasting pattern
of machine age images and outmoded architectural

Aircraft (1935)

monstrosities. At the end of *Croisade*, Le Corbusier specified
that the images paired with the architecture shots came from
the magazines *Vu* and *Voilà*, two French publications whose
illustrations relied heavily on photomontage.[8]

Published two years after *Croisade*, *Aircraft* is something
of an anomaly. As his only commissioned book (by the British
publishing house The Studio), its layout arguably stands out,
at least in part, as Le Corbusier's most modernist. Intended
as the first book in a series entitled *The New Vision* (named
after an expression coined by László Moholy-Nagy), *Aircraft*
reflects Le Corbusier's efforts to satisfy the requirements set
forth by The Studio for a style that would reflect the spirit of
the series (with, for example, bleeding full page photographs
and prominent page numbers). And there can be no doubt
that Le Corbusier was personally involved in the layout's
design, as the surviving correspondence between him and
the publisher indicates.

For the cover of *Des canons, des munitions? Merci!
Des logis... SVP*, Le Corbusier once again resorted to
photomontage, indeed to the same magazines which had

Des canons, des munitions? Merci! Des logis... SVP (1938)

provided the photographic material for *Croisade*. Here again, the political nature of the subject justified a visual vocabulary indebted to avant-garde graphic design. As the catalogue of Le Corbusier's and (his cousin) Pierre Jeanneret's participation in the 1937 Paris World's Fair, *Des canons* describes the origins and construction of their *Pavillon des temps nouveaux*, inviting the reader on a virtual tour of the site. Inside the book, Le Corbusier makes direct reference to photomontage techniques, specifically to those developed by Moholy-Nagy.

If, later on, Le Corbusier included photomontage in his published work – in particular to draw out connections between his architectural and artistic practices[9] – he still only very sporadically borrowed from modernist graphic design. In fact, he was just as liable to uphold the opposite aesthetic position. For example, regarding the American book *Quand les cathédrales étaient blanches*, published a year before *Des canons*, with what may be qualified as a photomontage on the cover, Le Corbusier warned the publisher: 'Take note, classical layout, no modernism please.' Already when Ozenfant and Le Corbusier were preparing to launch the magazine *L'Esprit Nouveau*, they made clear their intention to critique the Bauhaus, the 'elimination of capital letters' and Josef Albers' 'idiotic typefaces'. By contrast, Ozenfant's and Le Corbusier's project was 'to draw up a page of the typefaces we intend to use – legible ones.' Another symptom of this apparent anti-modernism was the virulent attack launched in the pages of *L'Esprit Nouveau* against the posters by the French graphic designer Cassandre for the furniture store Au Bûcheron, a commission that revolutionised the standards of urban advertising. Yet this attack owes less to artistic antagonism than to personal vendetta: at first the furniture store earned plaudits from the magazine's editors for its progressive campaign, but when it refused to buy advertising space in the magazine, Le Corbusier and Ozenfant sought (petty) revenge by authoring their scathing critique.[10]

The layouts of Le Corbusier's books from the 1920s have more in common with late nineteenth-century illustrated magazines than with avant-garde books. When the architect did stray from convention – as with the illustration in *Urbanisme* (1925), captioned 'Space reserved for a work imbued with modern feeling'[11] – it seems to be more in the spirit of Dada than of the Bauhaus.

Among other un-modern characteristics of Le Corbusier's published work is his preference for handwritten text and translucent coloured fields. These transformed the page into a space for artistic expression, rather than into an informational plane to be ordered according to a rational grid. Le Corbusier was first introduced to the technique and uses of these coloured fields by Pierre Faucheux, a young graphic designer who worked in his studio immediately after the war and whose influence on the architect's graphic design was considerable.[12]

To conclude, I would like to focus on a work that exemplifies what I believe is Le Corbusier's relationship to book production, namely *Les plans de Paris, 1922–1956*.

Les Plans de Paris, 1922–1956 (1956)

For the cover, Le Corbusier chose Chaillot, a typeface
designed by Marcel Jacno for the Théâtre national populaire
at the Palais de Chaillot in Paris, which the foundry Deberny
et Peignot had just released commercially. It is worth noting
that Jacno was also behind several type designs inspired by
cursive script – Scribe and Jacno – which belong to the
relatively anti-modern movement in France called 'graphie
latine' and which would have resonated with Le Corbusier's
affection for handwriting.[13] *Les plans de Paris* consists
almost exclusively of facsimile reproductions from Le
Corbusier's earlier books – including pages from his *Œuvre
complète* and *La ville radieuse*. Although Le Corbusier
reproduced and collected these pages without alteration,
he did intervene in the gaps and blanks in the composition
with handwritten text and areas of solid green. As soon as the
reader encounters the contents page at the start of the book,
the author urges her or him not to read the book but to cross
it: 'Reader, first follow the green track till the end.' *Les plans*

de Paris does not conform to an architecture in the way, for example, that certain Swiss designers advocated the use of a constructive grid as a matrix to organise printed information on the page. Instead, the book's form reflects the subject, becoming a stratified object as sedimented as the city it describes, made up layer upon layer of a motley assortment of buildings from different periods and in different styles. In the case of *Les plans de Paris*, Le Corbusier had no precedent, neither abiding by principles of modern graphic design nor opting for anti-modern ones. In this, Jacno's Chaillot offered an apt compromise: a stenciled type, slightly irregular and imprecise, but not as apparently hand-made as some of the main 'graphie latine' typefaces.[14]

Rather than as a compromise between truly modern and fundamentally anti-modern, could one not simply qualify Le Corbusier's approach to book design as postmodern? Postmodern, not in the negative sense sometimes implied by the term, but rather, to borrow from Kinross' introduction to the reprint of his *Modern Typography*, as Lyotard defined it against Habermas, that is, as dialectically related to modernism.[15] Close to Lyotard, Hal Foster's understanding of postmodernism in the visual arts – as a method of drawing from a repertory of forms – may in fact serve as a perfect description of Le Corbusier's approach to book production.[16] In the end, it may well be that France, which never embraced modern graphic design and unrelentingly sought an alternative typography – regardless of the motivations behind the proponents of 'graphie latine' (whose history, incidentally, remains to be written) – was, in terms of graphic design, the most hospitable terrain for a position such as Le Corbusier's. We may wonder, then, if what Kinross called France's 'marginality' would not be better described as an 'alternative way' – a way in which Le Corbusier stands as an exemplary case. Semi-modernity or postmodernity? The word is out.

1. Robin Kinross, *Modern Typography: An Essay in Critical History*, London, Hyphen Press, 2004 [1992], p. 97.
2. Le Corbusier, *My Work*, trans. James Palmes, London, The Architectural Press, 1960, p. 299.
3. Although Le Corbusier contributed to the volumes (published in Switzerland) that constitute *l'Œuvre complète*, he cannot legitimately be considered their author, editor or designer.
4. Among the magazines in which Le Corbusier's work appeared, see *Plans* (10 issues, 1931) and *Prélude* (16 issues, 1935–36).
5. Letter from Le Corbusier to Jean-Louis Ferrier, the director of the series at Gonthier, dated 10 July 1963 (Fondation Le Corbusier, E2-2-135).
6. Jan Tschichold, 'Qu'est-ce que la Nouvelle Typographie et que veut-elle?', *Arts et métiers graphiques*, no. 19, 15 September 1930, pp. 46–50.
7. See Gustav Klutsis, 'The Photomontage as a New Kind of Agitation Art,' in Margarita Tupitsyn (ed.), *Gustav Klutsis and Valentina Kulagina: Photography and Montage after Constructivism*, New York/Göttingen, International Center of Photography/Steidl, 2004, pp. 237–40.
8. The title of *Vu* was designed by Cassandre, and the magazine's art director at the time was Alexander Lieberman. Lieberman would later move to New York to become art director of *Vogue*, where his role in the visual transformation of women's magazines is well known.
9. See, for example, the special issue of *L'Architecture d'aujourd'hui* devoted to Le Corbusier, 1948. (See illustration above, p. 9)
10. *L'Esprit Nouveau*, no. 25, 1924, unpaginated. On the subject, see Anne-Marie Sauvage, *Cassandre*, exhibition catalogue, Paris, Bibliothèque nationale de France, 2005, pp. 38–39.
11. 'Place pour une œuvre de sentiment moderne.' *Urbanisme*, Paris, Crès, 1925, p. 38.
12. Faucheux went on to play a major role in the revival of the book in France, particularly with his designs for book club publications from the late 1940s and early 1950s.
13. On 'graphie latine', see Sébastien Morlighem, 'La Grafia Llatina i la creació tipogràfica a França (1949–61)', in *Crous Vidal i la Grafia Llatina*, Lleida, Museu d'Art Jaume Moreira, 2008, pp. 31–41, 293–98.
14. By using Roger Excoffon's Choc typeface for two of Le Corbusier's reprints, Jean Petit will side much less subtly with 'graphie latine.' See the dust jackets of *La Charte d'Athènes* and of *Entretien avec les étudiants d'architecture*, both published in 1943 (and republished in 1957) by the Éditions de Minuit in the Forces vives series directed by Petit.
15. Robin Kinross, *Modern Typography*, p. 9.
16. See in particular Hal Foster (ed.), *The Anti-Aesthetic: Essays on Postmodern Culture*, New York, New Press, 2002 [1983], and *Recodings: Art, Spectacle, Cultural Politics*, Seattle, Bay Press, 1985.

Image on p. 6: Detail of dust jacket of *Le Corbusier et Pierre Jeanneret – Œuvre complète*, designed by Max Bill (1934).

978-0-300-12395-1

9 780300 123951

PRINTED IN THE U.S.A.

re (Whitney/Yale) 2007

The Matta-Clark Complex:
Materials, Interpretation and the Designer

James Goggin

Consideration of materials appropriate for a given project
is a fundamental part of graphic design, particularly book
design. You could say that, when dealing with books, graphic
design crosses over into product design territory. Books are
three-dimensional objects of which the designer must consider
the aesthetic, functional and structural aspects. Effective use
of materials can succinctly communicate a book's content,
imbue it with a certain character and simply compel a reader
to pick it up.

An alternative title for this text might have been 'The
Temptations of Interpretation'. The temptations lie in the
vast range of materials the designer has at her/his disposal,
combined with the degree to which she or he chooses to
interpret a given content. How far one should go with the
interpretation of content through the choice of material
is a question I face with every project, particularly with the
art books that represent a large share of my commissioned
work. A key role of the designer is not only to take interest
in a book's content, but also to research and understand it.
Critical analysis of the content and application of this
knowledge usually result in a well-designed book, both
aesthetically and conceptually. But there is a fine line between
relevant, clever reference to the artist and more overt, less
helpful pastiche.

With particular artists, one risks reducing to parody
the very content of the book, or even blurring lines between
'the work' and 'the document'. The book should subjectively
communicate the work in a sympathetic way, but not
attempt to be the work, or risk being mistaken as such.
When designing a book, I aim to use relevant materials
in a measured way, but in spite of a general confidence
in my interpretation of the subject matter, there is always

an element of uncertainty: I always wonder if I have been thoughtful enough in the design. What might seem a knowledgable, referential solution to me might come across as unnecessary imitation to someone else.

Such concerns are exemplified by books on the American artist Gordon Matta-Clark, which I have been looking at for the past ten years. A cult figure in both architecture and art, Matta-Clark is best-known for what he called his 'building cuts' – works in abandoned buildings where he removed geometric sections of floors, ceilings and walls.

The design of books dealing with an artist often employs certain motifs or references to her or his practice: a certain material on the cover, a particular typeface for the text. I confess that I am by no means innocent of this, as such devices are often useful in communicating specific ideas of the artist's work. Books on Matta-Clark represent an ideal case study for investigating how far design should go in referencing art. Matta-Clark died prematurely in 1978 at the age of 35 and his ephemeral, site-specific work now exists only in documented form, particularly in books. This immediately sets up the potential for confusion between the artwork, its documentation and the book. Several books published posthumously on Matta-Clark mimic his interventions, or reference architectural materials from the artist's work in their construction (or *de*-construction) and typography.

The first copy of *Object to be Destroyed: The Work of Gordon Matta-Clark* (MIT Press, 2001) I encountered was actually the second edition: a paperback which could be described as an imitation of an imitation. This edition attempted, in flattened photographic form, to recreate the mix of flock pattern wallpaper and greyboard found on the original hardback cover. In both editions, the title on the cover is typographically cut across the two textures. The text pages are set in a more standard art catalogue format with serif type and generous margins, accompanied by the occasional angled title maintaining the cover's graphic device. The design approach here is to convey a rough idea

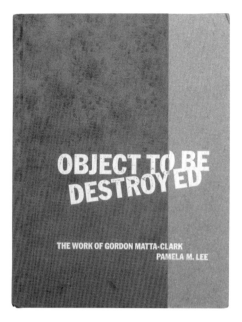

Object to be Destroyed: The Work of Gordon Matta-Clark (2001)

of Matta-Clark's work without use of archival imagery, communicating his method through treatment of material and typography.

My attention was recently, and belatedly, drawn to Linda Eerme's and Robin Kinross' article on three other books on Gordon Matta-Clark's work (*Domus*, 2003, no. 863). Published as part of a regular collaborative column by Eerme and Kinross, the article covered two earlier Matta-Clark books before moving on to the then recently published, lavishly produced *Gordon Matta-Clark* (Phaidon, 2003). This title marks the point where books on Matta-Clark went from subtle referential nod to a more overt form of reference, bordering on caricature. Eerme describes a situation where the book's designer 'is unable to resist the temptation to enter into competition with the artist'. The cover board, featuring Matta-Clark's *Splitting* (1974), has a large chunk taken out of the spine, exposing signatures embellished with ostentatious coloured thread. This original hardcover edition is admittedly

Gordon Matta-Clark (2003)

eye-catching, impressively executed and, we can assume, commercially successful (the edition is now sold out). And one could argue that the dramatic spine-cut was a striking way of bringing the artist's work to the attention of a wider audience. On the other hand, there is a danger that the motivation behind Matta-Clark's building cuts is trivialised if used merely as a decorative device.

In designing and producing his own book to document *Splitting* – published by 98 Greene Street Loft Press in 1974 – Matta-Clark was content to let the dramatic work speak for itself. The simple cover is set in a sans serif typeface with, inside, sets of overlapping photographs of the artist's architectural intervention.

In *Walls paper* (Buffalo Press, 1973), another book by Matta-Clark, the publication itself becomes an in-situ work, where his cutting process is not used to mimic the piece but to replace it. The building documented in *Walls paper* was demolished before Matta-Clark could return to halve it, so he halved the book instead. The reader 'splits' the building with each turn of the page.

SPLITTING

BY

GORDON MATTA-CLARK

Splitting (1974)

James Goggin

Walls paper (1973)

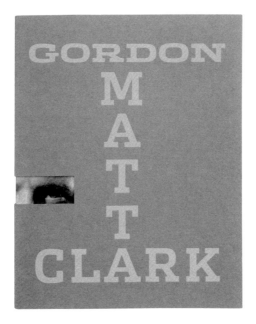

Gordon Matta-Clark: You Are the Measure (2007)

In *Gordon Matta-Clark: You Are the Measure* (Whitney/Yale, 2007), the most recent Matta-Clark book on my shelf, the book's designer also makes cuts: here in the kraft board cover, exposing a tightly-cropped portrait of the artist. The explicit reference, almost imitative, is still there, but manages to move beyond parody with the self-contained material play between die cut, photography and typography. One cut seems to approach tongue-in-cheek functionality: witness the neat void left for the all-important barcode. (See illustration p. 22)

As a parallel, questions similar to those raised by the Matta-Clark books came up while I was co-designing a book with Sara De Bondt, *DJ Simpson: Selected Works 2000–5*, which featured the work of British artist DJ Simpson (Mead Gallery, 2007). Simpson is also known for a method of subtraction, whereby a router is used to 'draw' by drilling lines across various surfaces such as plywood, aluminium, Formica and perspex.

DJ Simpson: Selected Works 2000–5 (2006)

Noting that a previous book on Simpson had mimicked the artist's mark-making with a scrawl-like headline font, we attempted a set of what we thought were subtler references. Headings and essays were set in fonts derived from plotting and engraving typography – a lettering technique often used to drill into materials similar to Simpson's, but in a more uniform way. With our perspex cover, we aimed to communicate the tension between a pristine slab of shiny red plastic and Simpson's striking destruction of the same material documented inside. In hindsight, we were perhaps equally guilty of over-enthusiastic interpretation, of an attempt to compete with the artist. The risk of such an approach is that it begins to turn the book itself into an art object, rather than letting the art speak for itself through the book.

This last observation highlights a key dilemma: where does the designer draw the line between engagement with content and pure decoration? Although consideration of a project's content and context remains crucial, the question reminds us to consider the book itself as a functional object. The quality of a book's constituent parts can be prioritised, a particularly basic requirement that is surprisingly often overlooked by contemporary designers. Is the right glue being used for the binding? Does the book open easily – and stay open? Is it comfortable to hold for extended reading? Existing 'readymade' formats (trade paperbacks, children's books, dictionaries, etc.) can be more sensitive to the book's materiality than effect-laden coffee table books.

An awareness of over-interpretation needn't imply a kind of unattainable (and undesirable) objectivity, but rather a thoughtfully subjective approach, which does not involve second-guessing the artist. When content and materials are interpreted and combined in a balanced way, the result can be greater than the sum of its parts. A transformation of the given matter through a kind of elegant alchemy, rather than cut-and-paste pastiche.

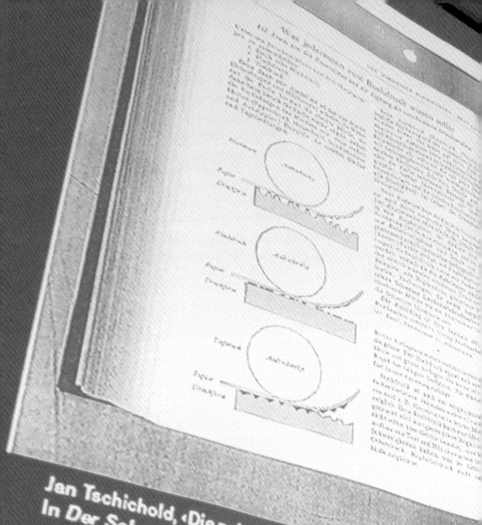

Jan Tschichold, ‹Die zehn schönsten Bücher des Jahres. Eine
In Der Schweizer Buchhandel, Nr. 15, 1943, p. 393.

1946, 1947, 1948:
The Most Beautiful Swiss Books in Retrospect

Jenny Eneqvist, Roland Früh & Corina Neuenschwander

Competitions rewarding beautifully designed books are enjoying increasing notoriety. They now exist in many countries, including Belgium, England, France, Germany, The Netherlands, Sweden and Switzerland. Every year, the winning entries of the national contests compete in The Best Book Design from All Over the World.

The Swiss competition, set up in 1943 by typographer and writer Jan Tschichold, was known in its time as one of the more conventional competitions, held in high regard within Switzerland and beyond. Its history is very well documented: the Swiss Federal Office of Culture, which organises the annual award, catalogue and exhibition, published *Beauty and the Book* in 2004 for its 60th anniversary. Yet despite this wealth of historical data, the fact that the competition was not held in 1946, 1947 and 1948 has never been discussed.

These three years represent a critical period in the history of Swiss book design, since by then the initial enthusiasm for Tschichold's New Typography had subsided, and the Swiss Style, or later International Style, had yet to emerge.

'1946, 1947, 1948' is a working title for a project that will form the basis of a lecture series, exhibition and publication. The project aims to (re)present significant Swiss books published between 1946 and 1948, independently selected by ten experts we invited. They set their own criteria and categories, without our or anybody else's input. What follows is an introduction to our project, its selectors and a first insight into some of their choices.

The Competition

The first record of a Swiss book competition is a short note by Tschichold, published in 1943 in the Swiss trade journal

Der Schweizer Buchhandel – a magazine to which he
regularly contributed at the time. In a brief paragraph entitled
'Die zehn schönsten Bücher des Jahres. Eine Anregung',
Tschichold refers to competitions in England and the United
States and suggests that a similar Swiss institution would have
a positive influence on the quality of national book design
and production.

> The competition will educate the public's taste, cultivate
> an interest in beautiful typography, book illustration
> and the like, and will certainly increase the sales of
> the rewarded books, which will again be seen as a
> motivation for publishers and printers to design their
> books with love.[1]

In March 1944, a jury declared 25 books – from among
approximately 250 titles – as the 'most beautiful'. But during
the first years of the competition, the jury's reports on the
submissions, published in *Der Schweizer Buchhandel*, were
rarely positive. To take a representitive example, Pierre
Gauchat, a graphic designer from Zurich, wrote in 1945 that
the submissions were 'rather uninspiring'. Even the rewarded
books represented 'more the average, than storm and stress'.
For Gauchat, the most beautiful book should satisfy the
following criteria:

> The typeface should not be too bold, and should ideally
> support the general character of the book. The type
> area is beautiful if it is (...) not too wide. A beautiful line
> contains 50 to 60 characters. The title should be set in
> the same typeface as the text. In general a thin book is
> more beautiful than a thick one.[2]

Tschichold entered the fray in 1946 with a long article
on the correct handling of a book's layout, paper, cover
material, format and typeface.[3] When he moved to England
later that year to work as a designer for Penguin, the
competition came to a standstill.

34

Historical Context

During the Second World War, publishers found themselves unable to satisfy the demand for books. At the same time, as a result of paper shortages, cheaper stock was used and more text crammed onto each page.[4] Publishers were also forced to print smaller quantities, and often wasted hours of labour having to reprint the same book over and over. This situation gave rise to the difficult choice between publishing new literature or reissuing old material.

Switzerland's neutrality in the Second World War contributed to its publishing boom for two reasons. First, unlike many European countries ravaged by the war, the Swiss publishing industry did not suffer from any interruption or major infrastructural damage.[5] Second, the Swiss book scene benefitted from the presence of immigrant designers such as the German Tschichold and the Hungarian Imre Reiner, two book design luminaries.

The Missing Years

While we may never be sure what led to the competition's interruption between 1946 and 1948, Tschichold's departure and the jury's disenchantment were no doubt compounded by the critiques of peers (published for the most part in *Der Schweizer Buchhandel*), who felt that the competition did not take into account such basic questions as: Does a common idea of 'beauty' exist? How many books should be rewarded? Should the jury pay equal attention to different types of books? And should jury members be free of personal and professional allegiances?

This is how the decision to abandon the competition was recorded in the minutes of the annual meeting of the association of Swiss booksellers:

Discussing the issue 'book competition' the assembly rejected to continue this institution, first established three years ago.[6]

We suspect that political circumstances played a role in this decision. At first, jury members were nominated as ambassadors for their respective trade associations (graphic designers, printers, bookbinders, publishers, booksellers, etc.), which at the time were organised in separate professional bodies. As a consequence of these bodies' importance gained during the Second World War, friction began to develop between them, each claiming to be under-represented in both the jury and the selection process.

It may well be that Tschichold thought better than to take part in these arguments, preferring instead to direct his efforts away from the promotion of good design. In the absence of his moderating voice, the dispute between the trade associations made it impossible for them to continue organising the competition. However in 1949, Gauchat brought the issue back to life by publishing a selection of statements in *Der Schweizer Buchhandel* for and against the idea of continuing the competition.7 Gauchat's persistence paid off: The Most Beautiful Swiss Books competition was held again in 1950 with eleven jury members, all of them trade association ambassadors, and has thrived ever since.

Methodology

We invited a group of experts from different fields of book production to make a selection of three to six items published between 1946 to 1948 and justify their choices.

- Peter Bichsel is the owner of an antiquarian bookshop in Zurich and curates book exhibitions.
- Julia Born is an independent graphic designer who teaches at the Gerrit Rietveld Academie, Amsterdam.
- Hans Burkhardt is the former director of the leading Swiss bookbindery Buchbinderei Burkhardt.
- Mirjam Fischer, formerly director of The Most Beautiful Swiss Books competition, now works for Edition Patrick Frey.

- Ursula and Jost Hochuli, typographers and graphic designers from St Gallen, made their selection as a team.
- Typographic designer François Rappo is head of Master Art Direction at ECAL/University of Art and Design, Lausanne.
- Christina Reble is responsible for publications at the Museum für Gestaltung, Zurich.
- Felix Wiedler, art historian, journalist and specialist of Richard Paul Lohse's work, granted us access to his extensive private library.
- Cornel Windlin is a graphic designer from Zurich, who currently chairs The Most Beautiful Swiss Books jury.

First Results

Bichsel nominated two books which, according to him, were ahead of their time and remain desirable, high-quality design objects. The first, published in 1948 by André and Philipp Gonin in Lausanne, is an illustrated edition of Jean de la Fontaine's *Fables choisies*. Bichsel cited its preciousness: a bibliophile artist's book printed in a small run of 300 copies, itself almost an artwork. Each copy bears the signatures of the artist Hans Fischer and the publisher.

Fables choisies (1948)

Bichsel's next choice, *Poètes à l'Ecart*, was published by Benteli in 1946. Edited by Carola Giedion Welcker, it is an anthology of out of print or unpublished poems by then up-and-coming writers and artists. Among these 'little known' figures are Wassily Kandinsky, Francis Picabia, Paul Klee, Pablo Picasso, Theo van Doesburg and Kurt Schwitters.

Wiedler chose the same book, for its strong constructivist design by Lohse and above all for its editorial quality. The book's design is an early example of the Swiss Style: square in format, its cover features an abstract, constructivist painting. The multi-lingual text is set in a single sans serif typeface in a limited number of point sizes.

The second art book selected by Wiedler is similar to *Poètes à l'Ecart*. The monograph and catalogue raisonné *Sophie Taeuber-Arp* (1948) was edited by Georg Schmidt, published by Holbein Verlag and designed in A4 format by Taeuber-Arp's close friend Max Bill. When looking at the book, what first stands out is the red title on the semi-transparent dust jacket, which, according to Wiedler,

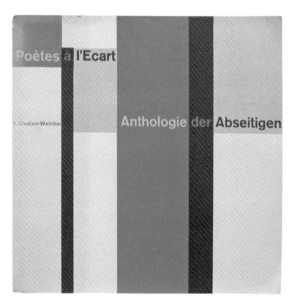

Poètes à l'Ecart (1946)

Sophie Taeuber-Arp (1948)

was a popular feature at the time. The book's design is
another example of early Swiss typography, but more
refined and elegant than Lohse's. The upright format and
unusual asymmetrical layout, combined with beautiful
colour lithographs contribute to its exceptional aesthetic
quality. Ursula and Jost Hochuli also aknowledged this
in their selection.

Wiedler's third choice – *Der Film: wirtschaftlich,
gesellschaftlich, künstlerisch* (1947) – also edited by Schmidt
and published by Holbein, has the same A4 format as
Sophie Taeuber-Arp. Hermann Eidenbenz was behind its
design, which is clearly influenced by New Typography.
The dominant, film-like grid structure on the book's cover
is applied throughout, a highly visual layout that prioritises
composition over legibility. Notwithstanding, Eidenbenz's
book remains an impressive object. To emphasise its
uniqueness, Wiedler compared it to the English edition,
which followed the same design but without the sans serif
typeface. Substituting the Swiss modernist type with a
more conservative serif blunted the book's radicalism.

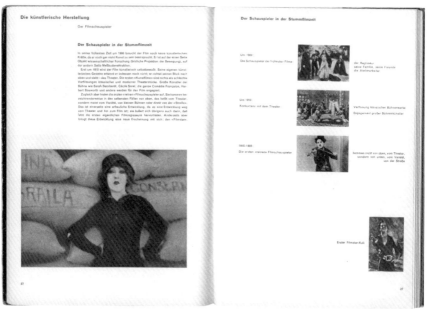

Der Film: wirtschaftlich, gesellschaftlich, künstlerisch (1947)

3
Nun seht ihr das Gesicht des
Tigers. Er ist froh und lacht,
weil er so schöne und weisse
Zähne hat. Es ist nur ein Bild,
aber es kann gut sein, dass es
eines schönen Tages lebendig
wird, nicht wie ein Spielzeug,
sondern richtig lebendig.

Urwald-Abenteuer (1946)

Ursula and Jost Hochuli chose more or less spontaneously
from their bookshelves, generally avoiding iconic artists'
books. Their first item is the German translation of the
children's book *Urwald-Abenteuer* (1946), written by the
Danish seven year-old Ileana Holmboe and published by
Holbein. The book, with its charming illustrations printed in
four vivid colours and two-colour display typography, stands
out from other books designed by Tschichold around this
time. Not only had Tschichold rarely used sans serif typefaces
for book design since the late 1930s, he had also written
about the misuse of such New Typography. Nonetheless,
for *Urwald-Abenteuer* Tschichold used a sans serif typeface

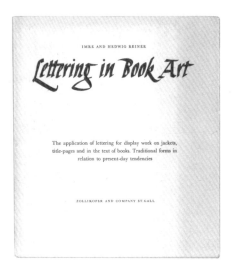

Lettering in Book Art (1948)

in a symmetrical layout throughout the book. This oversized typography was suited to its young readers, while giving the book a unique character.

Another choice by Jost and Ursula Hochuli was a book co-edited and co-written by Imre and Hedwig Reiner, under the deceptively simple title *Lettering in Book Art* (1948). The book's subtitle, however, offers a more accurate description of the work: 'The application of lettering for display work on jackets, title-pages and in the text of books. Traditional forms in relation to present-day tendencies.'

The book combines elaborate etched and wood engraved illustrations with an understated design. Zollikofer, the St Gallen publisher known for its high quality books, produced this as well as of six other titles by Imre Reiner, all of them dedicated to signage, lettering, or book illustration. *Lettering in Book Art* is a fine example of their collaboration: with its honest and elegant typography, the layout accommodates the many illustrations needed for the book's educational purpose.

The third selection by Jost and Ursula Hochuli is a small publication of about 30 pages – *Gedenkausgabe der Werke, Briefe und Gespräche* (1947) – a collection of guidelines for the production of the complete edition of Johann Wolfgang Goethe's works, letters and conversations. The complete edition, published by Zurich-based Artemis Verlag, eventually numbered 24 volumes. Jost and Ursula Hochuli suggested that Max Caflisch, the well-known Swiss typographer, was responsible for the layout of the book, which is exceptional both for its outstanding form and its detailed instructions for the future collection's design and layout. The precision of the information is impressive, with notes on typographic details as well as production (paper, binding and printing): as such, it constitutes a valuable example of a rare category of publication.

One book in particular reappeared on several shortlists: *Wir Neger in Amerika* (1948), published by the Büchergilde Gutenberg and designed by Lohse. The text is a translation of Richard Wright's novel *Twelve Million Black Voices: a Folk History of the Negro in the U.S.* Felix Wiedler, Jost and Ursula Hochuli, Christina Reble and François Rappo

Wir Neger in Amerika (1948)

43

Weißer Herr

Schwarze Tänzerin

10

11

Schwarze Arbeiterin

ein, bis hinunter zu den Vettern neunten und zehnten Grades. Aus einem Grunde, den wir nicht erklären können, sind wir mächtig stolz, wenn wir jemanden treffen, sei es Mann, Frau oder Kind, der uns im Gespräch eröffnet, daß er auf irgendeine Weise das Blut unserer Sippe in den Adern trägt. Da uns der Hunger nach Besitz nicht blendet, sind wir ein duldsames Volk. Eine schwarze Mutter, die unter der windschiefen Türe ihrer Lebkuchenhütte steht, wird wohl weinen, wenn sie ihre Kinder in die unbekannte Welt hinauswandern sieht; aber was sie auch tun mögen, was ihnen auch zustößt, was für Verbrechen sie begehen, was auch die Welt von ihnen denkt — wenn sie zurückkehren, wird die Mutter sie immer mit einem unwandelbaren menschlichen Gefühl willkommen heißen, das jenseits von Gesetz und Besitz liegt. Unsere Wertskala ist eine andere als die der Welt draußen, von der wir ausgeschlossen sind; unsere Schande ist nicht ihre Schande und unsere Liebe ist nicht ihre Liebe.

Unsere schwarzen Kinder werden uns in dem einzigen Raum, aus dem unsere ganze Hütte besteht, geboren, vor dem knatternden Holzfeuer, während rostige Scharen in Blechtöpfen kochen, die schwarze Plantagenhebamme hin- und hergeht, die Flammen der Fichtenscheite hohe Schatten an die Holzwände werfen und der Wasserkessel auf dem heißen Herde singt... Wenn unsere Kinder größer werden, sind sie uns eine tägliche Hilfe; sie holen in Eimern Wasser vom Bach, sie sammeln Holz, sie fegen den Boden, sie hüten die kleineren Kinder, sie rühren die Wäsche im schwarzen Waschhafen, der hinten im Hof über dem Feuer hängt, und sie buttern mit großem Eifer...

64

Manchmal ist für unsere Kinder ein halb verwittertes, tannenes Schulhaus vorhanden; aber selbst wenn die Schule das ganze Jahr offen stünde, hätten sie doch keine Zeit, sie zu besuchen. Wir können sie nicht von den Feldern fortlassen, wenn die Baumwolle darauf wartet, gepflückt zu werden. Wenn es Zeit ist, die Grasnarbe umzubrechen, dann muß sie umgebrochen werden; wenn es Zeit ist, den Samen auszulegen, dann muß der Samen gelegt werden; und wenn es Zeit ist, die rote Erde rings um die hellgrünen Stengel der Baumwollpflanze zu lockern, so muß auch das getan werden, selbst wenn es September ist und die Schule beginnt. Hunger ist unsere Strafe, wenn wir gegen die Gebote der Königin Baumwolle verstoßen. Die Jahreszeiten sind die Form, in die unser Leben gepreßt ist, und wer kann die Jahreszeiten ändern?

In unserm tiefsten Innern mißtrauen wir auch den Schulen, welche die Herren des Bodens für uns bauen, und wir haben nicht das Gefühl, daß sie wirklich uns gehören. In vielen Staaten sind die Herren des Bodens selbst Herausgeber der Schulbücher, aus welchen unsere Kinder lernen müssen; und in diesen Ausgaben lassen sie dann alle Stellen weg, in denen von Regierung, Abstimmungen, Staatsbürgerschaft und Bürgerrechten die Rede ist. Viele von ihnen sagen, Französisch, Latein und Spanisch, das seien keine Sprachen für uns, und sie werden wütend bei dem Gedanken, daß wir mehr lernen möchten, als sie uns erlauben wollen. Sie sagen: «Ein Nigger braucht nur gerade so viel Geographie zu kennen, daß er den Weg von seiner Hütte bis zum Pflug findet.» Sie haben es leicht, unsere Ausbildung zu

65

Wir Neger in Amerika (1948)

all cited the book's outstanding quality, making it a true icon of Swiss design. Three asymmetrically arranged black squares on a brown cloth cover refer to the grid that structures the entire book, allowing for striking contrasts between pictures and text, symmetry and asymmetry, black and white. The photographs are placed within the grid, but change position on every page, creating an almost cinematic experience. For the text, Lohse restricted the design to a single sans serif typeface set in the same size and weight throughout – a characteristic that would later be associated with Swiss typography. However, the atmosphere that *Wir Neger in Amerika* evokes comes mainly from its photogravure printing process. Even though it might render the text slightly out of focus, the process allows the text and the photographs to interact and gives an intense contrast to the images.

Conclusion

Our project is still in its infancy, but the initial findings already indicate what the final selection will look like. The selectors proposed not only specialist art books, but also a range of mass market publications, from a popular children's book to a typical art catalogue. Each of the shortlisted items could be the starting point for an in-depth discussion of issues of production, style, content and editing. For example, *Urwald-Abenteuer* forms a counterpart to Tschichold's classical style and sheds new light on the typographer's work.

By presenting the final book selection to the public we aim to highlight the significance of this missing period in the history of Swiss graphic design. Moreover, by reactivating the subjective selection process of The Most Beautiful Swiss Books competition, this project hopes to generate renewed interest in ways of thinking about, and evaluating, contemporary and future book design.

1. Jan Tschichold, 'Die zehn schönsten Bücher des Jahres. Eine Anregung', in *Der Schweizer Buchhandel*, no. 15, 1943, p. 393.
2. Pierre Gauchat, 'Die 25 schönsten Bücher des Jahres 1944', in *Der Schweizer Buchhandel*, Heft 8, 1945, pp. 181–84.
3. Jan Tschichold, 'Bemerkungen zur Auswahl der schönsten Schweizer Bücher des Jahres 1945', in *Der Schweizer Buchhandel*, Heft 17, 1946, pp. 561–64.
4. Gordon B. Neavill, 'Publishing in Wartime: The Modern Library series during the Second World War' published in *Library Trends*, Winter 2007, Johns Hopkins University Press and the Graduate School of Library and Information Science, University of Illinois at Urbana-Champaign, p. 586. http://www.ideals.uiuc.edu/handle/2142/3714?show=full [consulted January 2009].
5. Robin Kinross, *Modern Typography: An Essay in Critical History*, London, Hyphen Press, 2004 [1992], p. 146.
6. Die Redaktion, 'Buchhändlertagung in Einsiedeln', in *Der Schweizer Buchhandel*, Heft 11, 1947, pp. 341–42.
7. Pierre Gauchat et al., 'Zur Frage der Buchprämierung', in *Der Schweizer Buchhandel*, Heft 22, 1949, pp. 773–78.

BOOKS FOR OUR TIME

Ways of Seeing Books

Richard Hollis

Exactly sixty years ago, a series of meetings took place in Chicago to discuss 'the arts in relation to the book', out of which came the book *Graphic Forms* (Harvard University Press, 1949). Echoing the views of his pioneering friend László Moholy-Nagy, the book's main contributor, Gyorgy Kepes, proposed that the designer:

> Rethink the book functions in their physical, optical and psychological aspects. A book has weight, size, thickness and tactile qualities, qualities which are handled by the hand, as its optical form is handled by the eye ... The book can be conceived of in the same sense as the handle of a tool or a utensil ... and with perfect control.[1]

Only after this discussion of the needs of the hand does Kepes go on to talk about the needs of the eye, and of the reader's mind behind the eye.

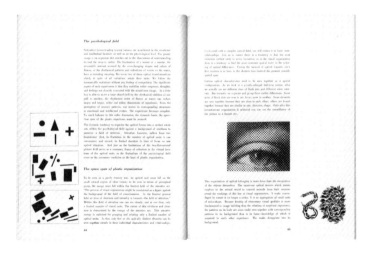

Language of Vision (1944)

49

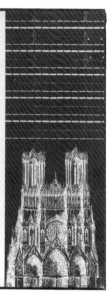

Despite considerable effort during the past thirty years to evolve a style of book design in the spirit of contemporary aesthetics and technology, the prevailing criterion of judgment is still the hand-printed-and-bound books of pre-Industrial Revolution eras... books which reflect the culture of their periods.

It seems incongruous that today, in a world of mechanical and material resources undreamt of in those days—a world finding expression in Stravinsky, Picasso, the UN Secretariat building and the products of our best industrial and advertising designers—we should yet strive to design books with conventions perfected centuries ago.

Our aim should rather be to evolve a contemporary expression—related to our world as the "traditional" style was related to its. This is an arduous process and the ultimate form of our books cannot be foreseen with certainty—but enough has been achieved already to demonstrate that we actually have valid new standards.

The book is not only a part of the world created by advertising, radio, motion pictures and television—it must compete with them for attention. To enable it to do so we must turn our eyes ahead, not backward, in designing the books of today.

Books for our Time (1951)

The first illustrations to Kepes' article are of his book *Language of Vision* (Paul Theobald, 1944). This publication is also reproduced in *Books for our Time* (Oxford University Press, 1951), which accompanied the exhibition of the same name in New York at New Art Circle Gallery. In the endpapers of *Books for our Time* the editor states that:

Despite considerable effort during the past thirty years to evolve a style of book design in the spirit of contemporary aesthetics and technology, the prevailing criterion of judgement is still the hand-printed-and-bound books of pre-Industrial Revolution eras... books which reflect the culture of their periods.

It seems incongruous that today (...) we should yet strive to design books with conventions perfected centuries ago. (...) we must turn our eyes ahead, not backward, in designing the books of today.[2]

In short, the form of the book has not changed significantly over the centuries: sheets of paper, printed on both sides, folded, trimmed on three edges and fastened together on the fourth with a cover. Once a craft, book making has become an industrial process. Today's mass-market paperbacks even retain the conventions of title page and contents divided into chapters. And the standardisation and success of this form of printed text, its ability to convey a narrative and give it a structure and sequence, has been frustrating to designers. They are left with little scope for invention.

Apart from a few typographic eccentricities, it was not until the modernist upheavals in the years after the First World War that the book's effectiveness in an age of mass media (and of the illustrated weekly magazine) was questioned. But the various historical avant-gardes – Futurists, Dadaists, Russian Constructivists, the Bauhaus masters – did not challenge the physical form of the book. They wanted to extend the ways in which the page could 'speak' to the reader. They were asking for its graphics to be updated, with such slogans as Moholy-Nagy's: 'Typography is the communication of ideas through printed design.'

Another reproduction in *Books for our Time* is a spread of Moholy-Nagy's *Vision in Motion* (Paul Theobald, 1947), published in the year after his death in Chicago. Writing in *Offset, Buch und Werbekunst* (1926), he had expressed puzzlement that:

> The majority of our books today have come no further in their typographical, visual, synoptical form than Gutenberg's productions, despite the technological transformation in their manufacture.[3]

Moholy-Nagy did his best to break with the traditional layout of film scripts in his *Painting Photography Film* (Albert Langen Verlag, 1925), a book full of wild contrasts between words and images. The later *Vision in Motion* uses a more sober style, but deploys the main text, images and extended captions in the same way as illustrated magazines, allowing

Vision in Motion (1947)

the reader to 'operate' in two ways. First, to skim through, looking at the pictures and captions and, second, after this familiarisation with the book's general ideas, to settle into the text.

Sixty years later, book design has become a largely conventional affair, in the hands of publishers (at least in the UK) who often resort to low production standards. At the same time, for better and often worse, it has become a medium for extravagant image-making. Kepes would be astonished by the way contemporary designers deal with a book's 'weight, size, thickness and tactile qualities'. Indeed, these characteristics often overpower the most admired books today. Dutch designer Irma Boom, well-known for a small book of more than 2,000 pages – almost as thick as it is wide and weighing 3.5 kilos – has had to concede that 'the contents of that particular book are so much more interesting than the look of it'. Such fashionable gigantism is typified by Bruce Mau's *S,M,L,XL* (The Monacelli Press, 1995), a huge portfolio for the author-architect Rem Koolhaas and his ideas.

S,M,L,XL (1995)

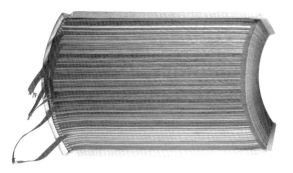

SHV Think Book 1996–1896 (1996)

Mau also designed a series of books for the Getty
Foundation. One is an 850-page volume of essays by the art
historian Aby Warburg, who was the subject of a farewell
lecture given by fellow art historian Ernst Gombrich. When
the latter arrived at the lecturn, on which lay the Mau-
designed tome, he slapped his hand down on the book
and declared, 'This book is too big'.

With fewer than 500 pages, Gombrich's best-known book,
The Story of Art (Phaidon, 1950) is comfortable to hold,
printed letterpress on coated paper. The illustrations appear
where they are needed in the text, making this book one of
the first 'integrated' books, since at the time plates were usually
located at the back, separated from the text. Phaidon, the
original publisher, reissued *The Story of Art* in 2006 as a

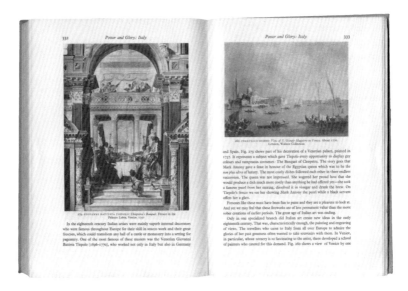

The Story of Art (1950)

pocket-sized paperback with more than 1,000 pages, elegantly produced and typeset, and expertly printed. For this edition, Phaidon returned to the old ways, with text at the front and plates at the back, printed on a slightly heavier paper. No longer does the story unfold. To link the words to the images, the reader is asked to juggle backwards and forwards with the help of woven bookmarks. This edition – and there were sixteen before this 'pocket' edition – is the first in which Gombrich was not involved in the layout. As he explained in the preface to the 1971 edition, the original book was:

> Planned from the outset to tell the story of art in both words and pictures by enabling readers as far as possible to have the illustration discussed in the text in front of them, without having to turn the page.[4]

This aim was achieved through 'weeks of intense collaboration', which included, Gombrich wrote, 'making me write another paragraph here or suggesting another illustration there'.

The Story of Art (2006)

The case of *The Story of Art* underscores the book's central role as go-between in conveying the author's meaning to the reader. And the most rewarding way to ensure that the go-between has understood the message is for author and designer to work together. Of course, a plain text only presents the designer with the task of making it readable and fit into the smallest number of pages, while at the same time meeting Kepes' requirements for the hand and the eye.

For several years, I worked with the writer and art critic John Berger, starting with a novel entitled *G* (Weidenfeld & Nicolson, 1972). Berger's typewritten text used line spaces rather than indents to indicate paragraphs. This spacing was retained in the typesetting, despite the problem that if a paragraph ends at the bottom of the page, the reader does not know if a new paragraph has begun. Berger also left larger gaps in the text to indicate a change of location or time passing. The typewritten copy was marked up with instructions for the typesetter, since the book was to be printed letterpress. The long galley proofs that came back from the printer were then cut up and the strips of text pasted up, page by page, with precise measurements for placing the type and chapter numbers (there were no chapter titles). These pages became the next printer's instruction. Sitting next to Berger, I felt no awkwardness in asking him if he could cut some lines at one point or if space could be added at another.

Another book I made with Berger was *A Seventh Man* (Penguin, 1975). Because the type was filmset, photoprinted galleys were pasted up on pre-printed grids, leaving empty rectangles for photographs which we selected as the pages were constructed. As with Gombrich and *The Story of Art*, text and illustration are closely integrated. But in the case of *A Seventh Man*, the images are not so much illustrations – they are as essential as the text.

This integration goes further in *Ways of Seeing* (Penguin, 1972). The book is based on a television series in which Berger's on-screen commentary was addressed either directly at the viewer or as a voice-over accompanying the image of

The migrant takes with him his own resolution, the food prepared in his home, which he will eat during the next two or three days, his own pride, the photographs in his pocket, his packages, his suitcase.

Yet his migration is like an event in a dream dreamt by another. As a figure in a dream dreamt by an unknown sleeper, he appears to act autonomously, at times unexpectedly; but everything he does – unless he revolts – is determined by the needs of the dreamer's mind. Abandon the metaphor. The migrant's intentionality is permeated by historical necessities of which neither he nor anybody he meets is aware. That is why it is as if his life were being dreamt by another.

A Turk: 'For six months a year in the countryside you sleep because there is no work and you are poor.'

At some point he crossed the frontier. This may or may not have coincided with the geographical frontier of his country. It isn't the geographical frontier that counts: the frontier is simply where he is liable to be stopped and his intention to leave thwarted. On the far side of the frontier, when he has crossed it, he

43

driver asked to see his money. A policeman was standing near by. Both policeman and taxi driver agreed that to go to the shanty town of Saint-Denis the passenger must pay double. He did not ask why. He was a newly arrived migrant who could not afford not to take a taxi and could not afford to argue. He too had crossed the frontier.

From Istanbul the majority of migrants go to Germany. Their crossing of the frontier is officially organized. They go to the Recruitment Centre. There they are medically examined and undergo tests to prove that they possess the skills which they claim to have. Those who pass, sign a contract immediately with the German firm which is going to employ them. Then they get into a labour train and travel for three days. When they arrive they are met by representatives of the German firm and taken to their lodgings and the factory.

46

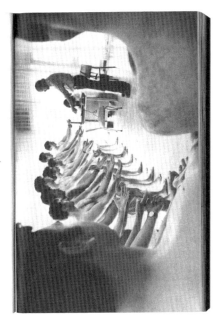

A Seventh Man (1975)

57

Richard Hollis

Page 26:

When a painting is reproduced by a film camera it inevitably becomes material for the film-maker's argument.

A film which reproduces images of a painting leads the spectator, through the painting, to the film-maker's own conclusions. The painting lends authority to the film-maker.

This is because a film unfolds in time and a painting does not.

In a film the way one image follows another, their succession, constructs an argument which becomes irreversible.

In a painting all its elements are there to be seen simultaneously. The spectator may need time to examine each element of the painting but whenever he reaches a conclusion, the simultaneity of the whole painting is there to reverse or qualify his conclusion. The painting maintains its own authority.

26

Page 27:

PROCESSION TO CALVARY BY BRUEGHEL, 1525–1569

Paintings are often reproduced with words around them.

This is a landscape of a cornfield with birds flying out of it. Look at it for a moment. Then turn the page.

WHEATFIELD WITH CROWS BY VAN GOGH, 1853–1890

27

Page 106:

Nevertheless the special relation between oil painting and property did play a certain role even in the development of landscape painting. Consider the well-known example of Gainsborough's Mr and Mrs Andrews.

MR AND MRS ANDREWS BY GAINSBOROUGH, 1727–1788

Kenneth Clark¹ has written about Gainsborough and this canvas:

At the very beginning of his career his pleasure in what he saw inspired him to put into his pictures backgrounds as sensitively observed as the corn-field in which are seated Mr and Mrs Andrews. This enchanting work is painted with such love and mastery that we should have expected Gainsborough to go further in the same direction; but he gave up direct painting, and evolved the melodious style of picture-making by which he is best known. His recent biographers have thought that the business of portrait painting left him no time to make studies from nature, and they have quoted his famous letter about being 'sick of portraits and wishing to take his Viol de Gamba and walk off to some sweet village where he can paint landscips', to support the view that he would have been a naturalistic landscape painter if he had had the opportunity. But the Viol de Gamba letter is only part of Gainsborough's Rousseauism. His real opinions on the subject are contained in a letter to a patron who had been so

¹ Kenneth Clark, *Landscape into Art* (John Murray, London)

106

Page 107:

simple as to ask him for a painting of his park: 'Mr Gainsborough presents his humble respects to Lord Hardwicke, and shall always think it an honour to be employed in anything for His Lordship; but with regard to *real* views from Nature in this country, he has never seen any place that affords a subject equal to the poorest imitations of Gaspar or Claude.'

Why did Lord Hardwicke want a picture of his park? Why did Mr and Mrs Andrews commission a portrait of themselves with a recognizable landscape of their own land as background?

They are not a couple in Nature as Rousseau imagined nature. They are landowners and their proprietary attitude towards what surrounds them is visible in their stance and their expressions.

Professor Lawrence Gowing has protested indignantly against the implication that Mr and Mrs Andrews were interested in property:

Before John Berger manages to interpose himself again between us and the visible meaning of a good picture, may I point out that there is evidence to confirm that Gainsborough's Mr and Mrs Andrews were doing something more with their stretch of country than merely owning it. The explicit theme of a contemporary and precisely analogous design by Gainsborough's mentor Francis Hayman suggests that the people in such pictures were engaged in philosophic enjoyment of 'the great Principle ... the genuine Light of uncorrupted and unperverted Nature.'

107

Ways of Seeing (1972)

58

a painting. On occasion there was an image without sound – this silence translated on the page as blank space. In fact, this interaction between word and image was hardly new, having been perfected in the 1930s by John Heartfield, among others.

In *Ways of Seeing*, a bold typeface grants the same weight to the text as to the images – unlike traditional popular art histories, which the reader can treat like a coffee-table book, scanning the pictures, glancing at the captions. To avoid distracting from the flow of argument, the captions in *Ways of Seeing* are limited to simple identifications running vertically alongside the images.

The original *Ways of Seeing* was a more or less standard paperback production of the early 1970s. It is now re-issued by Penguin Books in a series called *Modern Classics*. In a smaller format, repaginated, the cover reworked, without a title page but with the preliminary pages at the back – including the essential 'note to the reader' – underinked on heavier paper with the grain across the page, far from easy to open, or 'operate', the book at least reflects the culture of its time: an abuse of new technology under market-driven pressure. In the worst sense, a Modern Classic.

Where production values are so low, the arrival of new technology, such as the Sony Reader and Amazon Kindle, may at least satisfy Kepes' demands for 'a utensil' 'with perfect control'.

1. Gyorgy Kepes et al., *Graphic Forms*, Cambridge, Mass., Harvard University Press, 1949, p. 8.
2. Marshall Lee (ed.), *Books for our Time*, New York, Oxford University Press, 1951, endpapers.
3. László Moholy-Nagy, *Offset, Buch und Werbekunst*, Leipzig, 1926, no. 7, reprinted in H.M. Wingler, *The Bauhaus*, Cambridge, Mass., MIT Press, 1969, p. 80.
4. Ernst Gombrich, *The Story of Art*, London, Phaidon, 1971, preface to the 12th edition, reprinted in *The Story of Art*, London, Phaidon, 2006, pp. 11–12.

A Conversation with Bob Stein
from The Institute for the Future of the Book

Sarah Gottlieb

Sarah Gottlieb: Tell us about how you started? Where did the idea come from?

Bob Stein: The MacArthur Foundation approached me to get involved in publishing projects with CD-ROMs. I wasn't really into their ideas, since they did not correspond to the network era I felt we were entering, so I proposed the Institute for the Future of the Book. After some consideration they . agreed to endorse the project and were extremely generous with their funding.

What were the first projects you did with the Institute?

We hired some bright young people with strong backgrounds in the humanities and literature. For a year we discussed ideas about the future of the book in relation to networks and then just started doing experiments in this area.

In 2005 we began working with Mitch Stevens, a professor at New York University. We made a blog for him called *Without Gods*, about the issue of atheism, where he posted daily thoughts. Over the course of a year he gathered a very active group of readers, thinking through ideas with him.

The next project was with Kenneth McKenzie Wark, a media theorist at the New School in New York. He had written *A Hacker Manifesto* for Harvard University Press (2004). We built an online version of his new book *Gamer Theory* (2007), a critical reflection on video games. We made a breakthrough in its graphic design by taking the readers' comments and placing them next to the text instead of at the bottom of the screen. This small move made a huge difference, conceptually, because suddenly the writer and the reader were occupying the same plane, flattening the

traditional hierarchy of print. It was very exciting to suddenly
see them sharing space.

This was our most important discovery, in the sense
that it generated a lot more experimentation, all of which
confirmed the basic notion that a book is a place where readers
and authors can congregate. Reading and writing have always
been social experiences, but when frozen into print these
relations tend to be omitted. A significant book gets people
talking in society, but this is not seen or incorporated in the
paper-based object. What we've been working on is expanding
the boundaries of the page, to consider its social aspects, which
are so fundamental to it. We are re-defining content to include
the conversation that it engenders.

**Considering these two early interactive experiments, I am
wondering about the word 'book'. Do you think these projects
fall under the category of blogs or books?**

I think we are in a transitional period where these definitions
are up for grabs. We are now able to call a broad range of
things books. Every once in a while, one gets a glimpse of a
future that is not so strongly tied to the past. Take electronic
book readers, which emulate a two-dimensional book
experience. To think that this is the future of reading would
be a mistake. We are in a process of inventing the future by
re-inventing the past. But the future is probably not going to
look anything like that.

**Do you work with designers in the same way as you work
with writers, authors and readers?**

We worked with Rebecca Mendez, head of the design
department at UCLA. Rebecca designed *if:book*, and also,
crucially, came up with the name for it. A good designer is not
somebody who just does what you tell them to; a good designer
is someone who engages with the subject and comes up with
ideas you didn't have. *If:book* was a big success – the London
branch of the Institute was named after it.

Can you tell me about Sophie and why you produced this piece of software in 1992?

Everything made during the CD-ROM era involved serious design and programming skills. My feeling at the time was that in the long run we needed to erase the programming part to enable designers, editors and producers to work directly in the medium and not have to hand over content to programmers. We developed an assembly mechanism for rich media that could be used intuitively by designers and producers for layouts. We are now in a more advanced web era, and are familiar with what multi-modal documents mean. Sophie's importance, compared to its predecessors, is its network context; its documents are not only multi-layered but rich social experiences where readers occupy the page together and work together.

You have previously explained Sophie in terms of an online community book, because people could continuously add to the content. Is that correct?

Yes, people can add content in the margins. I believe that books are going to continue to evolve. If the author and readers remain actively involved, then the book's actual content will grow over time.

Why did you make Sophie an open source programme?

The Mellon Foundation, which funded Sophie, insisted on open source, so it could be accessed by the higher education sector and improved on by a community of users. The software has a better chance of developing over time with a large user-base than in a private corporation. Open source keeps you honest, and keeps you on your toes.

There is a need to be online to contribute to and interact with this knowledge. Do you think that this creates an elite, a limited group in society that will have access to these new forms of books?

Sure, of course it does. But publishing has always been limited, a lot of people cannot afford to buy books. Access is generally uneven, especially under capitalism, and will probably remain so. But that's not a reason not to go forward. The inner quality of these platforms is not technological but social – a social structure that reflects the one we live in.

The Institute for the Future of the Book

Mission

The printed page is giving way to the networked screen. The Institute for the Future of the Book seeks to chronicle this shift, and impact its development in a positive direction. The Institute is a project of the Annenberg Center for Communication at the University of Southern California, and is based in Brooklyn, New York.

Book

For the past five hundred years, humans have used print – the book and its various page-based cousins – to move ideas across time and space. Radio, cinema and television emerged in the last century and now, with the advent of computers, we are combining media to forge new forms of expression. For now, we use the word 'book' broadly, even metaphorically, to talk about what has come before – and what might come next.

Work and Network

One major consequence of the shift to digital is the addition of graphical, audio, and video elements to the written word. More profound, however, is the book's reinvention in a networked environment. Unlike the printed book, the networked book is not bound by time or space. It is an evolving entity within an ecology of readers, authors and texts. Unlike the printed book, the networked book is never finished: it is always a work in progress.

As such, the institute is deeply concerned with the surrounding forces that will shape the network environment and the conditions of culture: network neutrality, copyright and privacy. We believe that a free, neutral network, a progressive intellectual property system, and robust safeguards for privacy are essential conditions for an enlightened digital age.

Tools
For discourse to thrive in the digital age, tools are needed that allow ordinary, non-technical people to assemble complex, elegant and durable electronic documents without having to master overly complicated applications or seek the help of programmers. The Institute is dedicated to building such tools. We also conduct experiments with existing tools and technologies, exploring their potential and testing their limits.

Humanism and Technology
Although we are excited about the potential of digital technologies and the internet to amplify human potential, we believe it is crucial to consider their social and political consequences, both today and in the long term.

New Practices
Academic institutions arose in the age of print, which informed the structure and rhythm of their work. The Institute for the Future of the Book was born in the digital era, and so we seek to conduct our work in ways appropriate to the emerging modes of communication and rhythms of the networked world. Freed from the traditional print publishing cycles and hierarchies of authority, the Institute values theory and practice equally, conducting its activities as much as possible in the open and in real time.

From www.futureofthebook.org

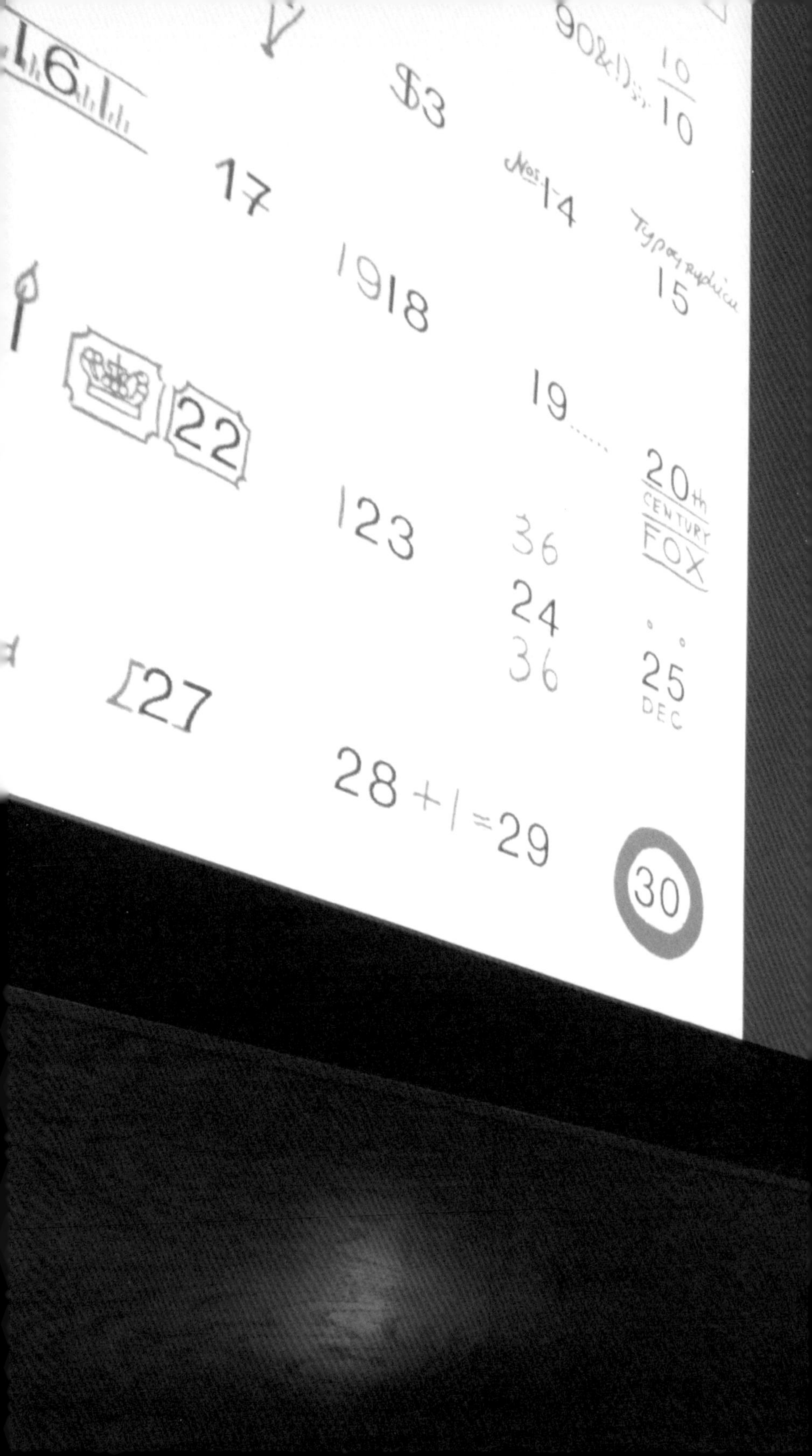

16.

$3

$90&!):₅ \dfrac{10}{10}$

17

Nos 14

1918

Typographica 15

19......

22

123

20th CENTURY FOX

36

24

36

25 DEC

27

28 + 1 = 29

30

Working with Herbert Spencer:
A Pioneer of Modern Typography

Chrissie Charlton

As a designer and typographer, Herbert Spencer's work encompassed book design, catalogues and corporate identities. But he was also a highly influential teacher and writer. In 1952, Spencer wrote *Design in Business Printing* (Sylvian Press) which included an in-depth analysis of paper sizes and typographic hierarchy. He edited and designed two series of the influential periodical *Typographica* (1949–59, 1960–67); edited *The Penrose Annual* (1964–73); and authored and designed *Pioneers of Modern Typography* (1969), which brought together the work of eminent pre-war European typographers and artists, among them Piet Zwart, Jan Tschichold, Kurt Schwitters, El Lissitzky, László Moholy-Nagy and Theo van Doesburg.

I worked as Spencer's assistant from 1971 to 1976, after studying Graphic Design at Hornsey College of Art in London. He had been our External Assessor and, much to my amazement, offered me a job. My approach to typography was rather 'psychedelic', and my knowledge of its mechanics minimal. Spencer had run his own design studio since 1947 with previous assistants including Alan Fletcher, Colin Forbes, Romek Marber, Alan Bartram and my immediate predecessor Hansje Oorthuys.

Before meeting him, I was expecting an austere character and discovered the opposite: a man with a mane of light red hair, a leonine beard and a twinkly disposition. On 6 October 1971, I started work in his basement studio at 30 Acacia Road, St John's Wood, London, at £15 per week.

Looking back at the material we produced over those five years, I am struck by how many books were printed in black and white, how many still used letterpress and the ghastly closeness between letters in the display typography.

First Steps

My first week was spent producing mock-ups for the
Frankfurt Book Fair, with the help of an ancient Océ
Skycopy wet copier, Pantone film and Letraset. The copier
used a developing fluid that only lasted a couple of days,
after which it exuded a vile odour. The prints eventually
faded, but for a short time produced a very graphic effect,
rather like the PMT (Photo Mechanical Transfer) cameras
of the late 1970s.

A typical day would begin with a briefing on the day's
or week's work ahead. Pat Gardiner, Spencer's long-time
secretary, would then arrive for three or four hours. Letters
were dictated and phone calls made. At around 1.45pm,
Spencer would leave in his grey Volvo for the Royal College
of Art, where he ran the Legibility Research Unit.

I spent most afternoons working on my own in the large
basement studio with its worm's eye view of the garden.
Occasionally a large tabby cat called Jeremy (who was the
spitting image of Spencer) would stroll by. At 2.30pm, his
Dutch wife Marianne would practise the piano until 4pm;
Schubert, Schumann, Chopin, Mozart and Beethoven
would make the time pass quickly and beautifully. Around
4pm their teenage daughter Mafalda would come home
from school. An hour later, Spencer would return to go
through the afternoon's work.

The first book I worked on was *New Alphabets A to Z*
(Watson-Guptill Publications, 1974), written by Spencer
and Colin Forbes of Pentagram, turning a Frankfurt Fair
mock-up into reality. The alphabets had been collected
from many contemporary designers including Block by
John Gorham, Expendable by Spencer's RCA colleague
Brian Coe, Oldenburg by Wim Crouwel, Peschici Stencil
by Silvio Coppola and Nudes by Anthon Beeke.

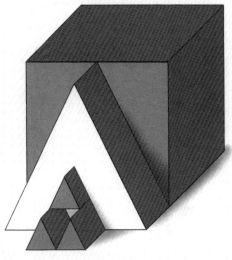

New Alphabets A to Z

Block
John Gorham

The designer of many vigorous and imaginative alphabets, John Gorham was commissioned by The Sunday Times magazine to prepare this set of initial letters for a special educational series.

Neon
Tom Carnase

A popular alphabet by one of America's most inventive lettering designers.

Tactile
Ron van der Meer

These letters were designed by van der Meer as part of a project for a set of children's building blocks so that the child could learn to 'trace' the shapes with his finger.

3D
Bob Gill

Many designers have attempted to create letters giving an illusion of a third dimension, but none has achieved this with a greater economy of means.

Jigsaw
John Gorham

An interlocking geometrically-constructed script, conceived as a three-dimensional educational toy.

Settembre
George Hoy

This contra italic alphabet was devised by Pentagram for use on an Olivetti calendar, and drawn by George Hoy.

Dance
Nick Jenkins

An effective use of the human figure as a basis for an alphabet, using a photographic technique.

Expendable
Brian Coe

Originally developed as an experiment to determine how much of each letter of the lower-case alphabet could be eliminated and the letter still remain legible.

New
Wim Crouwel

Designed particularly to satisfy the requirements of cathode-ray tube systems. Round shapes are avoided and only 45 and 90 degree angles are utilized.

Bodoni Stencil
WJHB Sandberg

Many posters and exhibition catalogues designed by Sandberg incorporate title lettering in this style, formed simply by eliminating the hair strokes of typefaces such as Bodoni.

New Alphabets A to Z (1974)

73

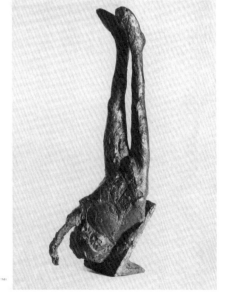

The Art of Elisabeth Frink (1972)

The next book was *The Art of Elisabeth Frink* (Lund Humphries, 1972), a monograph on the British sculptor. The experience was exciting as this book involved many meetings with the artist. The introductory essay and catalogue were printed letterpress on white laid paper; the photographs of her sculptures, lithographically on glossy art paper; and Frink's lithographs and etchings, on uncoated paper. I learned about the relationships of sculptures to each other, spread by spread, and the use of white space. The type was set in Univers (my first and probably only use of it), left-aligned, unjustified and generously line-spaced. I had to paste up galley and scatter proofs onto grid sheets with Cow Gum and make them fit in a certain number of pages – a number worked out previously in the book's flat plan.

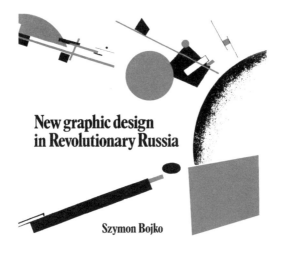

New graphic design in Revolutionary Russia (1972)

New graphic design in Revolutionary Russia (Lund Humphries, 1972), by the Polish writer Szymon Bojko, was a dream project for me, as it featured the work of El Lissitzky, Alexander Rodchenko and many other Russian Constructivists. Again I was learning about the relationship between image, text and captions. The book was set in

Monotype Grotesque and the versatility of this typeface with two weights produced an unobtrusive and understated layout within a square format.

Lund Humphries Printers and Publishers

Spencer had a long and fruitful relationship with both the printing and publishing arms of Lund Humphries. Established in 1895 by Percy Lund and Edward Humphries at The Country Press in Bradford, West Yorkshire, the company became one of the best fine art printers in Britain under their successors Eric Humphries and Peter Gregory. Their London office from 1932 to 1977 was in a fine Georgian house at 12 Bedford Square in Bloomsbury, in the basement of which Man Ray, Tschichold and Edward McKnight Kauffer would spend time in the 1930s. The works in Bradford housed Monotype keyboards and casters, and could print letterpress and offset lithography.

Spencer's relationship with Lund Humphries began after he approached Peter Gregory about *Typographica*, which he was then compiling. Gregory agreed to publish it, fearing the young designer would lose money on the venture. He also commissioned Spencer to rationalise the typefaces at the press, as well as produce a type specimen book and modern house rules for composition.

We often travelled to Bradford to check proofs, and I always felt a sense of exhilaration at the sight of the giant presses rolling. Spencer was very precise on colour and quality control, occasionally referring to a substandard proof as 'winkle bag printing'.

In 1959, Lund Humphries Publishers was established as a separate company where Spencer, John Taylor (previously at Macmillan) and Charlotte Burri (previously at Office du Livre) commissioned, edited and designed a series of monographs devoted mainly to British artists, including Henry Moore and Barbara Hepworth. The series would eventually grow to include books on architecture, design and typography.

The Penrose Annual (1970–73)

The major Lund Humphries publication with which
Spencer was involved was *The Penrose Annual*, which
he edited and designed from 1964 to 1973. Eminent
contributors such as Eric de Maré, Stefan Themerson,
Nicolete Gray, James Moran, Walter Tracy, Allen Hutt,
James Sutton, Alan Bartram, Jasia Reichardt, Emil Ruder,
Dieter Rot, Joseph Rykwert and Eckhard Neumann wrote
on a variety of subjects, such as computer typesetting,
design history and newspaper design.

The annual's A4 format was divided into three columns
and set in Times New Roman. Illustrations were often printed
on different paper as inserts, and gatefolds and wraparounds
gave a certain depth and texture. The spines and title pages
usually featured Spencer's favourite typeface – Standard
Medium – set in large letters. The 1972 cover featured an
alphabet based on Bodoni by Willem Sandberg, designer
and then director of the Stedelijk Museum in Amsterdam.

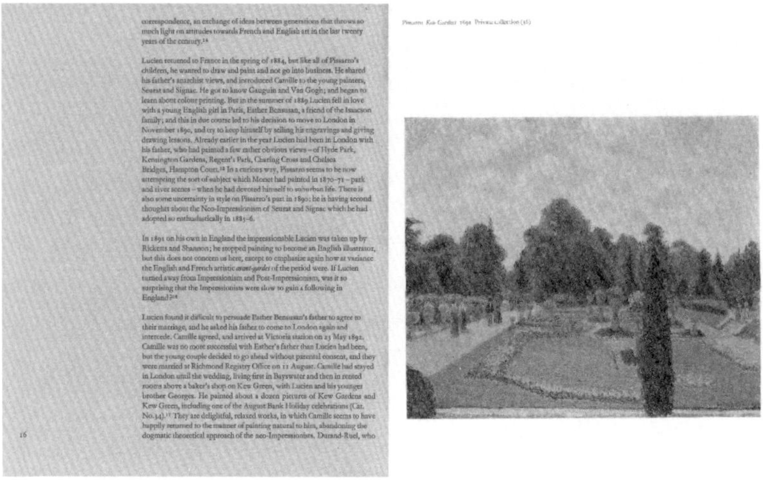

correspondence, an exchange of ideas between generations that throws so much light on attitudes towards French and English art in the last twenty years of the century.[14]

Lucien returned to France in the spring of 1884, but like all of Pissarro's children, he wanted to draw and paint and not go into business. He shared his father's anarchist views, and introduced Camille to the young painters, Seurat and Signac. He got to know Gauguin and Van Gogh; and began to learn about colour printing. But in the summer of 1889 Lucien fell in love with a young English girl in Paris, Esther Bensusan, a friend of the Isaacson family; and this in due course led to his decision to move to London in November 1890, and try to keep himself by selling his engravings and giving drawing lessons. Already earlier in the year Lucien had been in London with his father, who had painted a few rather obvious views – of Hyde Park, Kensington Gardens, Regent's Park, Charing Cross and Chelsea Bridges, Hampton Court.[15] In a curious way, Pissarro seems to be now attempting the sort of subject which Monet had painted in 1870–71 – park and river scenes – when he had devoted himself to suburban life. There is also some uncertainty in style on Pissarro's part in 1890: he is having second thoughts about the Neo-Impressionism of Seurat and Signac which he had adopted so enthusiastically in 1885–6.

In 1891 on his own in England the impressionable Lucien was taken up by Ricketts and Shannon; he stopped painting to become an English illustrator, but this does not concern us here, except to emphasize again how at variance the English and French artistic *avant-gardes* of the period were. If Lucien turned away from Impressionism and Post-Impressionism, was it so surprising that the Impressionists were slow to gain a following in England?[16]

Lucien found it difficult to persuade Esther Bensusan's father to agree to their marriage, and he asked his father to come to London again and intercede. Camille agreed, and arrived at Victoria station on 23 May 1892. Camille was no more successful with Esther's father than Lucien had been, but the young couple decided to go ahead without parental consent, and they were married at Richmond Registry Office on 11 August. Camille had stayed in London until the wedding, living first in Bayswater and then in rented rooms above a baker's shop on Kew Green, with Lucien and his younger brother Georges. He painted about a dozen pictures of Kew Gardens and Kew Green, including one of the August Bank Holiday celebrations (Cat. No.34).[17] They are delightful, relaxed works, in which Camille seems to have happily returned to the manner of painting natural to him, abandoning the dogmatic theoretical approach of the neo-Impressionists. Durand-Ruel, who

16

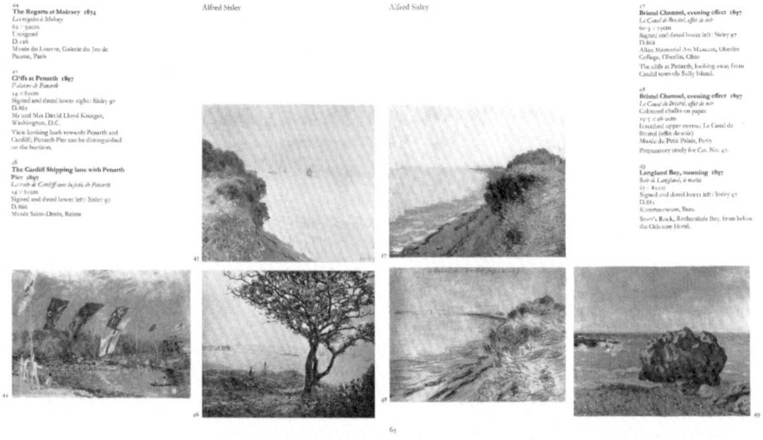

44
The Regatta at Molesey 1874
Les régates à Molesey
62 × 92cm
Unsigned
D.126
Musée du Louvre, Galerie du Jeu de Paume, Paris

45
Cliffs at Penarth 1897
Falaises de Penarth
54 × 65cm
Signed and dated lower right: Sisley 97
D.865
Mr and Mrs David Lloyd Kreeger, Washington, D.C.
View looking back towards Penarth and Cardiff; Penarth Pier can be distinguished on the horizon.

46
The Cardiff Shipping lane with Penarth Pier 1897
La rade de Cardiff avec la jetée de Penarth
54 × 65cm
Signed and dated lower left: Sisley 97
D.866
Musée Saint-Denis, Reims

Alfred Sisley

Alfred Sisley

47
Bristol Channel, evening effect 1897
Le Canal de Bristol, effet de soir
60·5 × 73cm
Signed and dated lower left: Sisley 97
D.868
Allen Memorial Art Museum, Oberlin College, Oberlin, Ohio
The cliffs at Penarth, looking away from Cardiff towards Sully Island.

48
Bristol Channel, evening effect 1897
Le Canal de Bristol, effet de soir
Coloured chalks on paper
19·5 × 26·2cm
Inscribed upper centre: Le Canal de Bristol (effet de soir)
Musée du Petit Palais, Paris
Preparatory study for Cat. No. 47.

49
Langland Bay, morning 1897
Baie de Langland, le matin
65 × 81cm
Signed and dated lower left: Sisley 97
D.881
Kunstmuseum, Bern
Storr's Rock, Rotherslade Bay, from below the Osborne Hotel.

65

The Impressionists in London (1973)

A memorable article included in the 1973 annual on the relationship between the different weights of Times New Roman, was illustrated by overlays printed on glacene paper. Also in the same issue were articles on fairground decoration by John Gorham and Geoff Weedon, and on Ben Shahn's underground press and lettering.

The first major art catalogue I worked on with Spencer was *The Impressionists in London* (Lund Humphries, 1973) for an exhibition at the Hayward Gallery, London. The cover featured a painting by Claude Monet, wrapped around the front and back covers, with no title except on the spine. Coloured laid paper was used for the text sections, with inserts for colour reproductions on glossy art paper, and a black and white illustrated section at the end. I learned about aligning pictures to the foot of the page, using overhanging figures for plate numbers, and about weights of typefaces, italics, non-lining figures and two- and three-column grids. The text was left-aligned, a major Spencer 'house style'.

Design Process

The design process has evolved considerably since the 1970s. In those days, our toolbox included tracing and layout pads, Rotring pens, blue pencils for drawing non-photographable grids, grid sheets for pasting up layouts, Cow Gum and spreader, lighter fuel for cleaning off Cow Gum, typescale, depthscale and casting-off sheets for calculating the number of pages a typescript would come to in a chosen typeface.

All type was set by commercial typesetting houses, either as galley proofs on a Monotype machine or by computer photosetting on bromide paper for large type sizes. Visuals were prepared by hand, using either Letraset or tracing type from specimen books.

As designers, we prepared a type specification and layout indicating typeface, size, measure and leading. Finished camera-ready artwork was prepared by cutting and pasting the bromides onto board with a transparent overlay indicating Pantone colours and tints. As photosetting was expensive, all corrections were made before final artwork was prepared – the designer's and the typesetter's roles were strictly defined.

Later Projects

I also worked on identities and leaflets, but book design still constituted the bulk of our workload. Spencer and his family would spend more and more time at their converted chapel in Powys, Wales, which he generously offered to my family and me for holidays. Workdays often flowed into enjoyable dinners with the Spencers' friends in the evenings. There was reciprocal cat-sitting, and the relationship was one of combined professionalism and friendship.

To conclude, I would like to briefly touch upon two projects from the later years. *Londoners* (Lund Humphries, 1974) was a book of monochrome photographs of north Londoners in their homes, taken by the young American photographer Nancy Hellebrand. The book required extensive preliminary editing with the photographer in order to achieve a rhythm of composition and subject matter. The titles and introductory essay were set in Modern No. 20 and Scotch Roman.

Londoners (1974)

Ivon Hitchens (1973)

We also worked on a large monograph and subsequent catalogue of the British abstract painter *Ivon Hitchens* (Lund Humphries, 1973). The plates were trimmed from large printed sheets and individually tipped in by hand on coloured paper.

In my last year with Spencer we designed a new handbook for the Imperial War Museum, a book of Henry Moore's war drawings and a Ceri Richards exhibition at the Edinburgh Festival. In the summer of 1976, Spencer became more involved with his academic work at the Royal College of Art, and after five years of working for him, it was time for me to leave. My first freelance job, which he helped me secure (a brochure on the house of architect Patrick Gwynne), and a day a week teaching at Watford School of Art, allowed me to embark on my own career, which continues today, almost 35 years on.

Spencer was my mentor, and my life as a designer would have been very different had he not spotted something in my psychedelic scribblings.

Herbert and Marianne Spencer at Runnis Chapel, Powys, in 1974

Every Book Starts with an Idea:
Notes for Designers

Armand Mevis

Every year around 400,000 new titles are presented at the Frankfurt Book Fair. Every time I hear this number I ask myself in disbelief: that many books in merely one year? And what about all the others that do not make it to the Fair? Though I have never been there, I imagine it as a hellish place you just want to run away from.

Out of all those books there must be only a few hundred whose design is worth looking at, fewer to talk about and fewer still to discuss in depth.

All these books have to be designed. Someone needs to decide which paper, typography, cover, to use. This is good news for designers: there is still plenty to do. It may be a jungle; you may find it hard to get the nice job, and you might get lost, but that is part of the adventure.

Looking back at the work Linda van Deursen and I made over the last 20 years, I count around 120 books, all of which fit on one shelf. Our whole career is just 100 inches wide, printed in small print runs.

Not all of these books have succeeded. We have learned by doing, as mistakes are inherent to the job of making books through trial and error. Sometimes, by pure luck, a book can come out well. Over the years we have learned to limit the number of mistakes; we are now much more in control. This does not mean that all our books are interesting. Some are even done too well, books where nothing happens at all.

Ideally, all books start with a question. The clearer the question, the more precise the answer, but this is rarely

Baghdad Calling (episode publishers, 2008)

the case. You have to find out what the question is. Sometimes those involved need to sit together for days, weeks, months before a book takes shape – and then I am not even talking about its design, but the shape of the content. As designers we are as responsible for content as anyone else.

Some books arrive in plastic bags like garbage, stacks of unsorted images on CDs, bits and pieces of writing, with no editor, no writer, no publisher and no money. Where to begin? Other books come almost ready-made, with the publisher having taken most design decisions, including dimensions, paper, binding and cover image. What's left for the designer is to make it all look good. How do you convince someone that this is not the way you want to work, that these decisions are an integral part of the design process? How can you make this situation more interesting, rather than simply rejecting the job?

But sometimes the conditions are ideal. You work with people who share your interests, with printers who do everything to get the book beautifully printed, and everything points towards a perfect solution.

Regardless of the initial circumstances, there are questions that need to be answered: What needs to be done? What are the main issues that need attention, the problems to be solved? What does not work, what is missing? How to create the right conditions for a workable situation?

Along the way you might need to fight for money, fight against expectations, fight for content, fight for fewer or more images, fight for readable text. Even when the situation appears promising there will always be messy parts that need to be resolved. You cannot just sit down and wait until it comes to you, because it will not come by itself.

To know how to solve things you need to be open, to reinvent, to rethink what a book can be. Rethink the form,

Barbara Visser is er niet (JRP|Ringier, 2006)

rethink how information can be organised, rethink the editing, propose alternative directions. From all this a book and its design will benefit. Designing a book is a collaborative process, the designer depends on others: all of you have to move together in the same direction. If the brief lacks clarity, be clear yourself. Ask the right questions, tell those you are working with what you think and need, explain your idea, get them involved.

All books start from their content. The content is a source of inspiration in itself, it tells you where to go. Understanding what the book is about is essential. Design and content need to go hand in hand, like a perfect dance. Sometimes there is too much design and not enough content, or the other way around: you need to find the right balance.

Even when you do nothing, you are doing something. Be aware of your decisions and what they mean for the book you are designing. You can make books better or worse. The content is the engine that leads to ideas, personal ideas, crazy ideas. Be clear about who you are, what you believe in and do not try to be someone else. Stick to your ideas. Embrace them. However impulsive or intuitive they might be, they are your treasures. Rely on the inner feeling that what you look for will work, that it will be right. Use your imagination to make the book that does not exist yet. It could be your best book ever.

All books tell stories about why or how they are designed. Some stories are good, sometimes even interesting. But every time unexpected problems occur and need a smart response – from rejected design proposals to technically impossible solutions – there is always drama. In the end these stories do not matter; what does is if a book actually works or not, that is, if you managed to get everything the way you wanted. If you were able to link the content to your concept and the concept to a form, you have succeeded.

Recollected Work: Mevis & Van Deursen (Artimo, 2005)

To find this form you are restricted on many fronts. First, there are technical restrictions. Almost all books are printed on paper. The printing technique is usually offset lithography; you can use black and white, full colour or Pantone colours. Not all dimensions for books are economical, as the size of books relates to the size of the printing machine and the size of paper it can handle. Books are bound in signatures of 4, 8, 16 or 32 pages. You realise that page 1 sits next to page 16 on a printing sheet. Paper has two sides, can be smooth or bulky. You always have to deal with the gutter in the middle of a spread. You can choose perfect binding, saddle stitching, soft or hard covers.

Besides technical restrictions you need formal skills. You can express your ideas through typography, page layout and the structure of information. Juggle these elements to find new combinations. In other words, make the best of restrictions. No matter what you do, in the end all books look like books, they don't look like buildings or cars, and amongst all 400,000 books at the Frankfurt Fair you will not find two books that look alike. Like fingerprints, they are unique.

This is the real challenge. Use your imagination, talent and skill to move successfully through the complexity of designing and making books. You need to dream about the books you would like to design, and this dream is what drives you; it is what keeps you going, wanting to do the next book and the book after that.

Biographies

Catherine de Smet

Catherine de Smet holds a PhD in art history. She teaches at l'École des beaux-arts, Rennes, and at l'École supérieure d'art et de design, Amiens. She is the author of numerous essays on graphic design and of two books published by Lars Müller: *Le Corbusier, Architect of Books* (2005) and *Vers une architecture du livre: Le Corbusier: édition et mise en pages, 1912–1965* (2007).

James Goggin

James Goggin set up his graphic design studio Practise in 1999, after graduating from the Royal College of Art, London. In addition to commissioned and self-initiated typographic and print-based projects, Practise designs exhibitions, signage, clothing, patterns and websites. Goggin is currently a tutor at the Werkplaats Typografie, Arnhem.

Jenny Eneqvist, Roland Früh & Corina Neuenschwander

Jenny Eneqvist graduated in 2009 from the Gerrit Rietveld Academie, Amsterdam, and now lives and works in London. Corina Neuenschwander graduated from Zurich University of the Arts and has been living in London since 2007, working for the studio Value & Service. Roland Früh graduated from the University of Zurich in 2007 and lives in London where he works for Hyphen Press.

Richard Hollis

Richard Hollis is a graphic designer, publisher and writer. He trained at various London art schools including Chelsea College of Art & Design and The Central School. He began his career as a printer, and taught at London College of Printing, Chelsea and The Central. He worked for Whitechapel Art Gallery in the 1970s, and since then has designed numerous books and art catalogues. He is the author of two books: *Graphic Design: A Concise History* (Thames & Hudson, 1994) and *Swiss Graphic Design: The Origins and Growth of an International Style 1920–65* (Laurence King, 2006).

Sarah Gottlieb

Sarah Gottlieb has lived in London since 2002. In 2006, she graduated from London College of Printing and two years later obtained her MA from the Royal College of Art. She is co-founder with George Wu, later joined by Dario Utreras, of Household, a design collective committed to collaboration.

Chrissie Charlton

Chrissie Charlton studied graphic design at Hornsey College of Art. From 1971 to 1976 she worked as an assistant for Herbert Spencer. She has been a visiting lecturer at Central St Martins, and at Kingston, Brighton and Northumbria Universities. Charlton now co-runs the letterpress design company Harrington&Squires with Vicky Fullick.

Mevis & Van Deursen

Armand Mevis and Linda van Deursen live and work in Amsterdam, where they began collaborating after graduating from the Gerrit Rietveld Academie in 1986. Their work has been shown in museums and educational institutions internationally. Van Deursen is head of the Graphic Design department at the Rietveld Academy, while Mevis is a design critic at the Werkplaats Typografie, Arnhem; both are critics at Yale University's School of Art, New Haven. *Recollected Work: Mevis & Van Deursen* was published by Artimo in 2005.

Sara De Bondt & Fraser Muggeridge

Sara De Bondt and Fraser Muggeridge run their own graphic design studios in London. De Bondt is visiting lecturer at the Royal College of Art, London. Muggeridge is visiting tutor at The University of Reading. In 2009, they co-organised The Form of the Book conference at St Bride Library, London, and co-edited *The Master Builder: Talking with Ken Briggs* (Occasional Papers, 2009).

Acknowledgements

Above all, we would like to thank the contributors who have been extremely generous with their time, effort and support, both in preparing and presenting their papers and transforming them into essays.

We would also like to express our gratitude to Catherine Dixon and Robert Banham at St Bride's for their invitation to organise the conference.

Thanks also to Antony Hudek for his editorial input, to Stephen Barrett for his assistance with the design, Sarah Newitt and Chris Svensson for proofreading and to Ella Finer, Ben Hillwood-Harris, Laurence Soens, Mafalda Spencer and Siôn Whellens for their support.

Special thanks to Calverts and Cassochrome for their printing sponsorship.

Colophon

The Form of the Book Book: essays by Catherine de Smet; James Goggin;
Jenny Eneqvist; Roland Früh & Corina Neuenschwander; Richard Hollis;
Sarah Gottlieb; Chrissie Charlton; Armand Mevis

Edited and designed by Sara De Bondt and Fraser Muggeridge
Copy edited by Antony Hudek
'Le Corbusier as Book Designer' translated by Antony Hudek

Inside front flap: Jan Tschichold, *The Form of the Book:
Essays on the Morality of Good Design* (Lund Humphries, 1991),
pp. 174–75.

Credits: pp. 6, 22, 32, 48, 62, 70 taken at The Form of the Book conference
by Jackson Lam; pp. 27–28 © Estate of Gordon Matta-Clark/Artists Rights
Society (ARS), New York, DACS, London 2009; pp. 6, 9, 14–16, 18
© FLC/ADAGP, Paris and DACS, London 2009, photographs by Luca
Ficcini; pp. 37, 39 photographs by Felix Wiedler.

First edition 2009
Second edition 2010

ISBN 978-0-9562605-7-4

Printed by Cassochrome, Belgium

Published by Occasional Papers
www.occasionalpapers.org
info@occasionalpapers.org

Distributed by
Central Books
+44 (0) 845 458 9911
contactus@centralbooks.com
www.centralbooks.com

Motto
+49 (0) 30 7544 2119
stores@mottodistribution.com
www.mottodistribution.com

Sponsor's Message

Cassochrome Graphic Production

A family business originally set up in 1973 with over 37 years experience in setting the highest standards for offset printing. By continually investing in the latest technology available, we have remained a market leader and the most energy efficient and environmentally friendly printers in Belgium.

Pre-Press
- Treatment and integration of all delivered data formats including; Certified PDF, QuarkXpress, Photoshop, Illustrator, Indesign and JDF
- Our newest CTP equipment is fitted with the finest digital workflow in the market for chemical free plates and all possible screens

Press
- Advanced S529 and S540, 5-colour KOMORI presses with dispersion varnish
- Sheet thickness from 60 gsm up to 1 mm (1/16 in)
- IR drying on both machines = consistent printing quality
- Water cooled inking rolls to ensure stability in the paper pile
- Online photo spectrographic measuring of the printing output

Constant communication throughout the process ensures each and every project achieves the best quality, on budget on time.

Please contact us for any information or advice on your printing requirements. We would welcome you to our offices to meet our team and see our equipment and examples of our work. Please contact Laurence Soens (laurence@csc.be) for more information

Quality is our goal!

Cassochrome
Oude Kassei 28, 8791 Beveren-Leie, Belgium
T +32 (0)56 73 83 93
www. csc.be